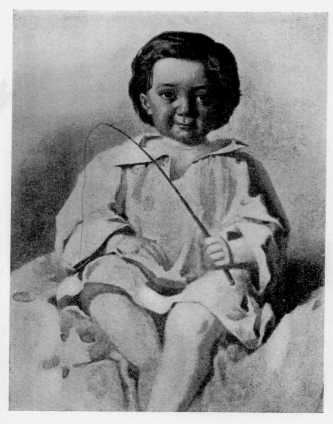

JOSEPH TEADOR KONRAD KORZENIOWSKI
AGED THREE AND A HALF YEARS.

From a photograph of a water-colour portrait in the possession
of a member of his family in Warsaw.

JOSEPH CONRAD
AS I KNEW HIM

BY

JESSIE CONRAD

". . . Ann, sister Ann, do you see anything
   coming?"
"I only see the sun that shines, and the grass
   that grows green."

Bluebeard.

LONDON
WILLIAM HEINEMANN LTD

First Published . . . *September 1926*
New Impression . . . *October 1926*

PRINTED IN SCOTLAND BY MORRISON AND GIBB LTD., EDINBURGH

TO

SIR ROBERT JONES
IN GRATEFUL AFFECTION AND REGARD

INTRODUCTION

FEW words from me are called for as introduction to this little volume of intimate and loving reminiscence. All who knew Joseph Conrad in his home knew how much he relied upon his wife's care and counsel, and how constantly his thoughts centred upon her. Her calm vigilance was ever on the alert to make the material things of existence as easy for him as possible, and to soothe the nervous reactions of his high-strung nature. Between them there was a deep bond of affection, and Conrad's anxiety as to his wife's health and as to her future when he should be gone was touching to witness. Often and often he had discussed these things with me into the small hours of the morning, and I know that they weighed heavily upon him. But if both of them worried over one another in secret, when they were together they would often talk in a vein of humorous and tender chaff, which was, in its own way, as sure a sign of their mutual devotion.

And therefore these reminiscences, fragmentary as they are, have a value all their own. Nobody else could speak with such authority, nobody else could give a picture so vivid within its scope, nobody else could relate so many personal facts. All future biographers of Conrad must turn to this book, and everybody who reads it will appreciate that the great novelist and master of our tongue was, indeed, fortunate in his marriage, and owed much to the heroic woman who shared his life for so many years, and who, though frequently herself in severe pain, tried always to hide it, if possible, from her husband, in order to shield him the better from worry and trouble.

RICHARD CURLE

PREFACE

ALL I have to say, the little stories I have to tell, will only throw into stronger relief the unusual, powerful personality of Conrad—a personality at once simple and complex.

Those of his friends who knew him intimately felt his charm, and even acquaintances came at once under his spell. Looking back over the years that stretch behind me, years we spent together, his sudden death seems to have been inevitable ; indeed, taking into consideration his indifferent health and nervous temperament, I marvel that he lived so long.

His whole attitude to life was opposed to any idea of rest ; he gave the impression of continual restlessness. A friend of his who had known him longer than I, told me that he had been always the same, even at sea : he was never still, never in repose, even when resting. It is perfectly true that he wore himself out. The end was like a long, breathless pause—a pause that seems to last still. I bitterly regret I was unable to be with him that long, last Saturday. The attack appeared identical with many previous ones, when I had always managed to calm him, to coax him into swallowing some light nourishment, and then watched beside him until he fell asleep—a sleep of utter exhaustion.

I will quote a letter he wrote to me on one occasion when I had to go to London to consult Sir Robert Jones. It will show what I shall often illustrate—Conrad's emphatic speech and intensity of feeling, even over trifles:

" . . . I have just got the wire in time to save me blowing the top of my head off with pent-up worry. All my sympathy for the little girl that is going to be put to bed for a fortnight. But I know you (of all women) are not going to be unreasonable about such a thing. Moreover, Sir Robert has spoken! That's enough. I wonder anxiously how much tired you are—and in what particular way—for you are a woman of considerable varieties. It is only your sweetness and the grace that are in your heart which are always the same.

" I worked all morning. Note for 'Secret Agent'[1] is finished *and* copied clean, 1.30. At 2 o'clock Dick wired that he was prevented

---

[1] The play taken from "The Secret Agent."

coming by the boy developing influenza. Wired back sympathy. You won't be surprised to hear that I couldn't sit at home twirling my thumbs while waiting for the wire. At 2.45 started for Hythe, nursing 3 wine glasses. Arrived 3.30. Old bandit very facetious pretending to drink strong waters from every pattern of glass in the shop. Left 4.5 *via* Folkestone with a dozen claret glasses confined in a box. Am now very frightened at the purchase. A cut-glass cup sat by my side on the back seat. Wants a job as a flower-holder in the window. Wages £3 10s. for ever. Arrived home 4.53. Tea. At 5.15 top of head lifting slightly. 5.29 wire. All pressure gone and a vague desire to go to bed and whistle tunes, but won't do that till after dinner. Great hugs for you and the boy. Love from your own property, J. C."

This letter and the following one, written on board the *Tuscania*, 21st April 1923, when on his way to America, will perhaps make people understand why I want so much to publish this little book of memories :

" MY DEAREST AND BEST,—I am writing this in my cabin on my own bit of paper, in great anxiety as to the news your wire to Moville may bring me, and feeling most remorseful at having left you in a state of suffering." (I was to have a painful examination of my knee, the result of which I was to wire in time to catch his boat at Moville.)

"I was met at Glasgow by Muirhead Bone, who has just done for you that pencil 'note' of a bit of the coast we have passed about half an hour ago. With him was John Bone and the Editor of the *Glasgow News*—an old friend—N. Monro. I gave them a dinner (excellent) at the hotel. Dick has been marvellously attentive—could not have looked after me better if he had been own son. Captain B. is delightfully friendly and the ship is fine. Weather very clear, a little cold, with an easterly breeze. You may rest assured I'll be well looked after. But I won't tell you I'll have a pleasant trip. I'll miss you too much. I will do my best to make the visit a success—for all your sakes. B. sent me a cheery wire this morning. Dick promised to wire you on getting ashore and to write you on Sunday.

"My breathing is better to-day, and the cough quite tolerable. I wish I could see and hear your voice. Thanks no end for the beautiful packing. I found everything to hand. You are a treasure! I will keep this letter open on the chance of adding two words more on receipt of your wire. It has been hard to part with John at the station. Give him a kiss from me. Your own property,

" J. C."

It has actually been asserted in print that Conrad hated the sea ; one reviewer even found that fact plainly visible in "Typhoon" ! But who could have proved his love of the sea more completely than Conrad ? It lives and speaks in his books. The following passage from "Life and Letters" shows clearly the spirit in which he became a seaman :

"At nineteen years of age, after a period of probation and training I had imposed upon myself, as ordinary seaman on board a North Sea coaster, I had come up from Lowestoft— my first long railway journey in England—to 'sign on' for an Antipodean voyage in a deep-water ship. Straight from a railway carriage I walked into the great city with something of the feeling of a traveller penetrating into a vast and unexplored wilderness. No explorer could have been more lonely. I did not know a single soul of all these millions that all around me peopled the streets. I cannot say I was free from a little youthful awe, but at that age one's feelings are simple. I was elated. I was pursuing a clear aim, I was carrying out a deliberate plan of making out of myself, in the first place, a seaman worthy of the service, good enough to work by the side of the men with whom I was to live ; and in the second place, I had to justify my existence to myself, to redeem a tacit moral pledge. Both these aims were to be attained by the same effort. How simple seemed the problem of life then, on that hazy day of early September in the year 1897, when I entered London for the first time. . . ." " All the help I had to get in touch with the world I was invading was a piece of paper not much bigger than the palm of my hand—in which I held it—torn out of a larger plan of London for the greater facility of reference. . . ." " I found my man at last, the man I had written to, my first letter in English. His business, he explained to me, was to find good ships for young gentlemen who wanted to go to sea as premium apprentices with a view of being trained for officers. But he gathered that this was not my object. I did not desire to be apprenticed. ' Of course I can see you are a gentleman. But your wish is to get a berth as an Able Seaman if possible. . . .' " He doubted that he would be able to help me in this. There was an Act of Parliament which made it penal to procure ships for sailors."

To a friend in Australia he wrote, when he was appointed to his first command—the barque *Otago* (1887)—whose captain had died on her passage out: " One day, all of a sudden, all the deep-lying sense of the exploring adventures in the Pacific surged up to the surface of my being. Almost without reflection I sat down and wrote a letter to my owners, suggesting that, instead of the usual southern route, I should take the ship to Mauritius by way of the Torres Strait. To my surprise they agreed, provided I was certain the season was not too advanced to endanger the success of the passage by the calms that prevail at times in the Arafura Seas. . . ." " The season being advanced, I insisted on leaving Sydney during a heavy south-east gale. Both the pilot and the tug-master were scandalised by my obstinacy, and they hastened to leave me to my devices while still inside Sydney Heads. The fierce south-easter caught me up on its wings, and no later than the ninth day I was outside the entrance to Torres Strait. . . . It was not without a certain emotion that, commanding very likely the first, and certainly the last merchant ship that carried cargo that way—from Sydney to Mauritius—I put her head at daybreak for Bligh's Entrance and packed on her every bit of canvas she could carry. Wind-swept, sun-

b

lit, empty waters were all around me, half-
veiled by a brilliant haze. . . . And thus I
passed out of Torres Strait before the dusk
settled on the waters. . . ."

The letter from which this extract is taken
was published in the *Sydney Mail*, 26th August
1925. It shows that Conrad was not merely
a literary man with a knowledge of the sea
and seamen. Such a creation as old Singleton
(suggested by a real character), is itself a proof
of this. Conrad had a great regard for all
followers of the sea ; indeed, he was particularly indulgent to any weaknesses betrayed by
seamen.

Once he insisted on my engaging a maid
simply because she was a daughter of an old
sailor who lived in Northfleet. He had inter-
viewed the father, who had assured him of his
daughter's efficiency, and I was quite prepared
to find her all I could wish. This experiment
proved one of the most exasperating of our
domestic adventures : the girl was a consum-
mate humbug. She once gave me a great
fright. Our eldest boy, a baby of nine months
old, lay asleep in his perambulator by the
garden door. Imagine my horror when, returning after an absence of fifteen minutes to
peep at him, I found the perambulator empty
and the child gone. At the moment I did not

connect the disappearance with the girl, who, as a matter of fact, had been granted the afternoon off. I was desperate, for I had heard no sound, no cry, nothing whatever to call my attention. Hurriedly we, Conrad and I, surveyed the fields surrounding the lonely farmhouse. There was scarcely a hedge in sight capable of hiding the child. An hour of this torture drove him nearly frantic, till shading my eyes with my hand I made out a figure carrying something some three fields off. We started hurriedly towards it. It was the girl with the child in her arms. Her only answer to our agitated questions was a silly giggle and an impudent " Don't care."

But I see I am already slipping into story-telling and forgetting that I am writing an introduction ; yet the very fact that I have done so will prepare the reader better than any preface of mine for what follows. For I am going to write just as though I were talking to a friend beside the fire ; searching my memory for those intimate recollections which others, who could draw a much more brilliant portrait of my husband, cannot supply. Many of them may seem trivial, but they may help the imaginative and sympathetic to know Conrad as he was.

CONTENTS

LIST OF ILLUSTRATIONS

JOSEPH CONRAD AS I KNEW HIM

I

CHARACTERISTICS

MANY friends and admirers have written understandingly about Joseph Conrad, but these recollections of mine should be the most intimate. I knew him for thirty-two years, and shared his life and fortunes for twenty-nine. He used often to say that I was no relation. At first this statement, though true, used to disconcert me not a little. My only consolation is the knowledge that my constant care enabled him to produce so fine a volume of work to stand as a perpetual monument to his memory and as a heritage to his sons. Many people have alluded sympathetically to his straitened means during his early writing life. There were many years too lean not to be without grave anxiety for us, but I will never admit that he suffered much in that way. His was not a happy nature, and he often anticipated trouble long before it came. On the other hand, he had a curious way of shrinking from actualities when it came to facing suffering. When this characteristic was first brought home to me I was taken aback and not a little frightened. But after some months in Poland, during the outbreak of war, I discovered that this temperamental peculiarity was characteristic of his nation. This discovery made it easier to understand him without making my concern too apparent, and to sympathise with his apprehensive anxiety. Our visit to Poland at the beginning of the war threw light back upon my early impressions of him, and provided me often with much food for reflection.

I like to remember that I was able to make those early writing years less trying than they might have been. I early developed a talent for cooking, and this made it possible for him to receive in his own home the friends he loved—friends who, one and all, generously welcomed me as one with him. He used laughingly to declare that Edward Garnett had greatly disapproved of his marrying at all. I have had many proofs that this—apprehension, shall we call it?—disappeared before Garnett had known me a week. It is curious, but I must myself have felt dimly from the first that there were good reasons why Conrad's friends should have dreaded marriage for him. It was not merely that he had already lived so many years as a bachelor, and had got used to life under utterly different conditions ; for him the hazard of marriage was so great for another reason. Few people could hope to understand him sufficiently to be happy in constant contact with a nature so charming, yet often hyper-sensitive and broodingly reserved. As one friend says, one always felt that there was a depth within him that after even years of the closest friendship, one had not reached. Before I had been married a week I felt that was true ; as a prospective bride I somehow knew in advance it would be so.

When we decided to live our lives together, I made fixed resolutions that I kept to the letter. I determined that his bonds should rest lightly on him ; that to all intents and purposes he should feel as free as if he had remained a bachelor. I never interfered in the slightest with his liberty of thought or action. This is why I held his trust and affection to the end. Indeed, he grew to depend on me much more than he himself was aware. In later years, when his clear judgment would be obscured by some little hurt to his personal pride—some

trifle he would obstinately regard as injurious
to the dignity of Joseph Conrad—which im-
pelled him to write a long letter of flowery
remonstrance or furious protest, I would wait
till he brought the letter to me. If I could not
approve, I handed the letter back without
comment. This always brought forth the
irritable question, " You don't say anything ?
Don't you approve ? " This was my opportunity. I could generally convince him that it
was unnecessary, and that a letter of protest
loses dignity if it contains a word too much.
I was always careful, however, to point out
it was only *my* opinion, and to suggest that
he probably knew better. This was usually
effective, for he was very proud of me —
his possession—his precious possession—as he
would often call me. He claimed to have had
from the first a profound insight into my character and an intimate knowledge of my capa-
bilities. I, on my side, used to tease him, and
declared that his choice of me was only pure
chance.

He was intensely proud of his two boys, but
he had an almost superstitious dislike of hearing
them praised by any one else ; and while
extremely generous to other people's children
he was always most reluctant to let his own
accept presents. Once, when the late Lord

Northcliffe, who had been lunching with us and had taken immensely to our small boy John, declared his intention of depositing five pounds to the boy's credit at an electric model shop, Conrad became quite distressed. In fact, I think the only time a present to the boys really pleased him was when M. André Gide sent a large box of Meccano. It came unexpectedly which no doubt accounted for its different reception. That present really gave as much satisfaction to the father as to the son. The two would spend hours together building some complicated bridge or crane, while I looked on, pleased and amused, thankful indeed to see my husband taking an interest in something else beside books. He would often say later on to me, " That boy is really quite intelligent, you know." I agreed instantly, of course, and never failed to point out that he ought to have a full share of intelligence. It was one real grief to J. C., as we called him in the family, that the boys, as he said, " had no literary curiosity and showed almost a dislike for printed matter." It was in vain I pointed out the difference between their childhood and his own : they had not been so dependent on books. And then in desperation I would suggest that perhaps they had inherited some of their characteristics from me, and that both would probably turn out men of action. This hardly consoled him. He would continue to lament that neither seemed fond of reading. " I could read French at the age of five," he would grumble. Both our boys had great difficulty in mastering that art even in their own language. Borys's progress through those early lessons was painful in the extreme, yet no one could doubt his intelligence. He could have been barely three when he astonished his father by laboriously nailing together a wooden sole for his gouty foot. Conrad treasured those pieces of wood for many years. He had them tied on over the thick bandages, after I had carefully blunted the tips of the nails, and the small boy's face would wear an expression of utmost satisfaction whenever his invention was brought into use. On one of these occasions he asked me, " Mama dear, when I'm a man, shall I have a little boy ?—and . . . shall I have the liver and the dout ? "

This child was the first infant Conrad had seen nearer than the width of a street, and his remark when the boy was presented to him was, " Why ! It's just like a human being." He certainly was, with his thick black hair parted on one side, his manly fists protruding from his elegantly turned-back cuffs, and that wonderful expression of wisdom peculiar to babies when they first enter this world—an expression which persuades mothers to credit them with some profound consciousness of their power to console and reward us for our sufferings. In the first moments of my pride and joy in my own baby, I recalled a story of Conrad's own infancy. While his parents were making that forced journey into political exile, the child fell desperately ill. His mother craved permission to interrupt their journey, and I shuddered at the brutal answer, " What's one baby's life among all these thousands ? If it is dying, leave it behind ! "

Conrad's earliest memories had graven indelibly on his childish mind a sense of tragedy.

As he says in the " Personal Record," his earliest recollection was of a bizarre, shabby travelling-carriage, with four post-horses, standing before the long front of his uncle's house. This carriage was waiting to take the child and his mother back into exile, where his father awaited them. Only by special favour had mother and son obtained permission to spend three months' leave in her brother's house. Here it was that Conrad learned to speak and read French ; the last injunction from his governess was, " N'oublie pas ton français, mon cheri." He never did.

Much of the real significance of that time

was, of course, missed by the child, but later on his uncle explained to him the whole sinister meaning of what had taken place. That uncle, to whom the small boy owed so much, must have tasted to the full the bitter dregs of helpless suffering—for instance, to know that his sister was seriously ill, too ill to travel, and then to have his petition for extended leave refused in the following terms, must have been almost unendurable. This is what happened.

By the kindness of a police captain, who had been serving for many years in the district, and was really humane, my husband's uncle was allowed to read the document refusing his plea. It was a service order, issued from the Governor-General's secretariat, dealing with the matter of the petition, and directing the police captain to disregard all remonstrances and explanations in regard to illness either from medical men or others, and if she had not already left her brother's house on the morning of the day specified on her permit, *she was to be dispatched at once under police escort direct* to the prison hospital in Kiev, where she would be treated as her case demanded.

The man stood wringing his hands and begging the brother, with tears in his eyes, to see that his sister left, whatever her condition, on the morning named in her permit ; and the small boy had wondered *why* an official was there to see the carriage drive away! Conrad has told me many times how he sat silent and greatly subdued by the side of that slight figure in deep mourning, his hand held fast in her slim fingers, during the long journey back to his father. I have in my possession a faded photograph of his mother's lonely grave.

Another recollection belonging to Conrad's early years, and one that I do not think has ever before been made public, he told me many years ago. After his father had been permitted to leave one place of exile for another on account of his health, and father and son were living together, his maternal uncle often tried to induce his father to part with the boy for the sake of his future. Conrad must have been then between ten and eleven, for it was only a short time before his father died. One night, a cold night, he distinctly remembered going to some sort of guard-house, near a railway station, and there meeting his father's brother, who was a hunchback and was travelling, either with or under escort, through the village where they were living. He drew a vivid picture of the two men in earnest converse all through the night. They had piled the grate high with smouldering logs and made the boy a bed of rugs and coats in the corner. Every time he opened his eyes, he saw them in the same position, their heads close together, still deep in serious discussion. When it grew light, his father roused him and bade him say good-bye to his uncle, telling him mournfully that his uncle was keeping all that remained of his inheritance in trust " for you my son." What became of that uncle Hilary, I never heard. Photographs of him are in Conrad's album—a book that accompanied him through all his wandering and adventurous life, and now lies beside me on the table. He always referred to it as " the grave-yard," and he was very reluctant to let any one see it. Once I sinned grievously by placing a photograph of one of the boys between its covers. " Don't put any one's photograph in that book, I beg of you ! " he said.

After the death of his father, Conrad returned to the house of his maternal uncle, and thus shared with his young cousin Josephine the loving care of his mother's favourite brother. He told me one little story of this time. It was in his uncle's house that for once in his life he became intoxicated. The two children had been playing together, and Conrad, left alone, wandered down into the empty dining-room. There had been a large luncheon party and the table was not yet cleared. He walked round, draining the glasses and devouring the remaining fruits and sweets that took his fancy, till, overpowered with a desire for sleep, he found his way into the ladies' cloak-room. There he laboriously climbed on to a large table and curled himself down among the cloaks. In Poland, guests must perforce remain many hours on a visit on account of the great distances between the houses. For some time he was not missed, and when he was, the hue and cry failed to disturb his heavy slumbers. It was not until a search-party was on the point of starting to explore the grounds, and grave anxiety began to be felt on account of the heavy fall of snow, that his hiding-place was discovered. Some of the guests anxious to leave and not embarrass a stricken household, while putting on their cloaks, discovered him asleep. His condition was deplorable, and it was not until the next day he was sufficiently recovered to explain the cause. He used to declare that he could remember the terrible feeling of sickness even all those years afterwards.

The following two occasions revealed him to me in a new light, and proved that he was even more complex than I had hitherto supposed. The sister of a maid we had—a child of four— died suddenly under somewhat tragic circumstances, and Conrad was greatly impressed. Nothing would satisfy him but that I should drive into Folkestone to order a fine wreath of flowers, and, further, provide trappings of woe for the parents. This I did, but I was entirely unprepared for the next development. He had been, as he sometimes called it, " under the weather,"—in other words, fighting an attack of gout, and he had kept his room for the last week. The morning the little child was buried, he commanded me to produce a complete suit of mourning as he intended to attend the funeral himself. This completely took me by surprise, and I ventured to argue with him more emphatically than I had done before. I pointed out that it was a wet day, that there was no time to get a trap of any sort, and that the churchyard was more than a quarter of a mile away. No argument could move him, and half an hour before the time fixed for the funeral, I watched him limping painfully out of the gate on his way to the village. He had perforce to be content with such black clothes as he had. In my mind's eye I see him now, clad in a long frock-coat, evening trousers, tall silk hat, and a home-made black tie, a strange figure among the cottage mourners clustered round the grave. He did not enter the church, and spoke only a few words of consolation to the parents.

This impulse of sympathy was the talk of the villages round for quite a long time, and the vicar tactlessly made a special call upon us to thank him for attending. I was fortunately able to prevent him from doing this by intercepting him at the gate. Conrad would have been furious. We never referred to this incident; I think he forgot it as soon as it was over. I still marvel at it myself, not so much at his conceiving the idea, but at his carrying it out at so much personal inconvenience; for while my husband was at all times mentally active, physically he was extremely indolent. Then, too, he shrank with an almost morbid sensitiveness from the sight of pain and distress. For instance, during the war we had some wounded soldiers to tea. While they sat round the table in the dining-room, feeding themselves as well as their bandaged limbs allowed, one and all expressed their pleasure at the prospect of meeting the man whose books had helped them through many hours of pain and discomfort. Naturally, I kept listening for the sound of my husband's footsteps on the staircase. They came at last, halted, and then the door-handle turned; I glanced round without calling the attention of my guests. Slowly the door opened a little wider, and I saw Conrad peeping through in his short-sighted way. A moment passed. I was on the point of speaking aloud when, with a gesture of horror, he flung up his arms and retreated rapidly and silently. He explained later with a shudder that he could not face the ordeal of sitting at the table with those poor human wrecks. " Perhaps Borys will come home like that ! " he whispered.

I suppose to a man of such vivid imagination those awful years during the war must have been even more intensely painful than to other people. The sight of his tortured face has often called forth all my maternal feeling, and at such moments he was to me a son as well as a husband. Neither of us would have lifted a finger to prevent our boy from doing his bit, and we lived, like so many other parents, on those welcome field-cards and rare letters. We were seldom apart; but once, when I had been away from the house for a few hours (on one of my many visits to see a surgeon, in fact), I was greeted on my return by a weeping maid. My startled " What is it ? " drew another burst of tears and a few whispered words I could not catch. To my question as to the whereabouts of my husband, the girl's answer struck me almost dumb. " Mr. Conrad is upstairs, Mum, in Mr. Borys's room. He's been there all day, ever since he told us . . ." " Told you what ? " " He says he knows Mr.

Borys has been killed, but we haven't had any telegram."

I made my painful way up the stairs (for I am very lame) and found him sitting by the book-shelves, aimlessly glancing at books and replacing them on the shelves. He looked up at my entrance, and came eagerly forward to know what Sir Robert Jones had said. "What's the matter?" I forced my dry tongue to articulate, my voice sounding to my own ears miles away. "Nellie tells me you have had no news!"

"Can't I have a presentiment as well as you?" he answered impatiently, and he added in a whisper, "I *know* he has been killed!" I saw that he was in no condition to be reasoned with. I could only soothe him as I would have soothed a child. Presently he grew a little calmer, and after a time he consented to eat something; soon he was sleeping soundly. I crept from the room and reassured the household, feigning an optimism I was far from feeling. Because he was in a weak state of health and alone, he had allowed his imagination to run away with him. It was about this time that I had pointed out that his dedication to "The Shadow Line" was somewhat misleading; it read as if our boy had been killed. Nothing, however, would persuade him to alter it. I know that in several instances distant friends have been misled by that dedication.

I have no doubt that the war brought back even more vividly than ever his tragic early life to his recollection, and I have a firm conviction that for a long time before his death he felt the call of his native land—though he was as good an " Englishman " as any born and bred, as loyal to her interests and as devoted to the English people. But I have always felt very strongly his dual nationality, and for this reason I have arranged to keep the flowers above his last resting-place in the Polish National colours, red and white.

Few artists are well fitted to deal with the ordinary difficulties of life, and Conrad had far too lively an imagination for everyday events. He lived life as a novel ; he exaggerated simple trifles, though quite unconsciously. But his imagination made him a wonderful talker. I have been amazed sometimes while hearing him talk and hold a whole roomful spellbound. In those days, before his voice became uncertain, before he grew to distrust it and in consequence to strain it till it was sometimes painful to listen to him, he would start off, spurred by some remark, and recall some long-forgotten incident out of the depths of his memory. He would pace the room, gesticulating in his usual picturesque manner, and his hearers would be very attentive and for the most part silent. But now and then perhaps some one would interrupt with a question ; this temerity usually called forth a more emphatic statement and still more energetic movements of the hands. Often and often I have sat and marvelled at the extent to which, in his mouth, the same story varied. Each statement, if the same in the main, would be entirely different in detail. I suppose, with a born novelist, the mixture of fact and fiction in narration does always tend to vary. Dates varied most. I have read and re-read his written reminiscences, and although I am never tired of them, in the printed page I miss those varying arabesques of detail.

Conrad had one very marked characteristic : he would allow no argument in his own family circle. In early days I often transgressed by attempting to correct his dates. I have heard him repeatedly give the date of our marriage as two years later than it was. At first I interrupted him eagerly, pointing out that our boy was born that year. He would turn quickly towards me, frowning his displeasure : " You will allow me, my dear, to know as much about it as you do. After all, he is my son as well as yours—besides, I never consider

2

you as old as that." Though this was not a very cogent argument, I had perforce to hold my tongue. It is a curious fact that in all his dated statements he is usually two years out. Everything happened two years earlier than he says, almost without exception. This has made it sometimes difficult for his biographers to place the facts of his life correctly.

So many memories crowd into my mind as I write, little incidents in themselves, but, now that he is here no longer, fraught with a new meaning for me and tender significance. Looking at John, so like his father in appearance, I recall Conrad's story of how, when he was an ordinary seaman before the mast, his captain's wife, moved by some sudden impulse, presented him with a cheese-rind. I can picture him receiving it with a charm of manner which must have disconcerted the good woman not a little—with a profound bow and military click of the heels. It was always difficult for me to reconcile the highly sensitive, fastidious man with the rough life he must have led in his sea-going days. In his later years he carried fastidiousness to a degree that bordered on the fantastic. Once a new maid, unaware of his dislike of having the joint on the dining-table, proudly placed before him half a calf's head. It was quite elegantly prepared, but unfortun-

JOSEPH TEADOR KONRAD KORZENIOWSKI
AND HIS YOUNGER SON
JOHN ALEXANDER KONRAD KORZENIOWSKI.
ZAKOPANE, 1914.

ately it looked what it was. He gave one disgusted glance at it, promptly reversed his chair, and sat with his back to the dish. It was impossible not to laugh. The poor girl was disconcerted almost to tears, and it required a great deal of tact and diplomacy on my part to keep the peace. I had the dish removed at once to my end of the table, and produced speedily the second course, which happened that day to be a macaroni cheese, a favourite dish of his. He at once turned his chair and began eating in high good humour. No further reference was made to the incident by either of us ; but when I could control myself sufficiently to keep a straight face, I recalled the girl and gave her a full explanation, taking the blame of the mistake upon myself. Had I not done so, I feel certain she would not have remained another day in the house.

Conrad had also a bad habit (acquired at sea) of making bread pellets and flinging them about the room ; sometimes they flew in such unfortunate directions that people might well have been forgiven for thinking themselves targets. I have seen them fly into the soup-plates and glasses of our guests. The more excited or irritated he got, the quicker flew the missiles, and those in the line of fire would look apprehensively at their host. Carefully choosing my time I pointed out to him that he *had* this reprehensible habit, and it was agreed between us that I should at such moments call his attention to it by saying something quite irrelevant to the subject of conversation. Once we had several American guests to lunch ; I think we numbered ten round the table. The talk had turned to railways and railway stations. At first I was deep in conversation with my neighbour over some family matter, and I did not notice the growing excitement of my husband, or the nervousness betrayed by my guests. Something had raised Conrad's ire with a vengeance. Bread pellets flew in all directions and with a rapidity that was vastly disconcerting to the whole table. One or two actually struck the maids serving lunch. I leaned forward from my end of the table, and made one or two ineffectual attempts to attract his attention. At last I caught his eye, and said distinctly, " Conrad, your tie is crooked." He half started from his chair, slapped his hand sharply on the table, and, frowning heavily, said in a tense whisper, " This, my dear, let me tell you, is not the time or place to talk about my personal appearance ! "

It was plain he had quite forgotten our compact, and each time I caught his eye he only looked sadly reproachful. Still, my object was accomplished; the tension was relaxed. When lunch was nearly over I caught a sudden smile on his face, and I saw he had at last realised the object of my remark.

Once John managed to run foul of his father, which was a very rare event. He was justly rebuked by a smack. (He was then a small boy of four or thereabouts.) This experience was new to him and I fear he did not appreciate the justness of it. I asked him, a little later in the day, to take his father the newspaper. His reply amused us for long afterwards. He looked solemnly at me and then said, " Mama dear, do you mind sending one of the girls, because to tell you the truth I am a little irritated with him." This incident goes a long way to show the quality of the friendship between the boys and their father. They, too, understood his queer whims and fancies.

For instance, the boys and I were quite prepared for him when he came into the room and found us reading. Conrad would invariably fidget and worry till you put down the book you were reading. He would then pounce upon it and return with it to his own study. This happened so many times that at last Borys hit upon the idea of laying down his book when his father entered and picking up another.

Sure enough his father would worry about the room till the book Borys held in his hand was laid aside, when it was carried off in triumph. With a wink at me, the boy would then resume the book he was really reading.

Once, when we were in town together, I was told off to secure rooms in the hotel where we usually stayed. Conrad, as he had some business, arranged to join me later. (I remember vividly his comic disgust while relating what had happened to him, in the interval.) His business over, he had walked rapidly into another hotel and curtly requested the waiter to " tell my wife I am here." The waiter's very natural question, " What name, sir ? " had exasperated him, and he had answered sharply, " Mrs. Conrad, of course." When the man returned after a short absence with the information that there was no one of that name in the hotel, Conrad called for the manager, and now, greatly irate, turned on him tensely with the command, " Produce my wife ! " It was with difficulty he was persuaded that he was in the wrong hotel.

During those early years of writing, when he would sit far into the night, I always prepared a supper-tray in the next room for him. He would enjoy that meal immensely, and he never failed to do justice to whatever had been placed before him. At other meals he was always ready up to time, for unpunctuality in his eyes was a grievous sin. He insisted on variety, and he had no patience with any one who professed indifference to food. Once I made him very angry by spending a trivial sum on some rose trees. He reproached me bitterly. " Ah ! don't talk about it, my dear ! Three pounds for those sticks and not a damned rose in the garden ! " He ignored my defence that it was April, too early for the trees to flower.

II

FIRST DAYS

I WAS the second child of a family of nine, leading a quiet life of circumscribed interest in a quiet, remote part of greater London; and my marriage, apart from the momentous change it always implies, had also for me an added element of high adventure. I was to leave England for a prolonged period, to live far away from all those whose very thought and intentions were to me as an open book; I had to endeavour to adapt myself to the moods of a man whose mind had been occupied with the meaning of life, with its difficulties, joys, and sorrows, long before he had met me, an utterly inexperienced girl of twenty-two. From the first I did not think that I could understand him completely. But he seemed to understand me very well. There was one thing I felt certain of, and that was that we were starting on our joint adventure with a very real and profound affection between us, and with trust in each other. And I may say that already on my part there was, even then, a great deal of maternal feeling for that lonely man who had hardly known anything of a mother's care, and had no experience of any sort of home life.

We were married on the 24th of March 1896. It was a very fine day. We have often agreed since, when talking over the past and apart from all sentimental feelings, just as a matter of positive fact, that it was one of the most beautiful days that we could remember in our lives. But by the time we got down to Southampton, on our way to Brittany, the weather had completely changed. We dined in a large hotel near the docks, in a very splendid but practically empty dining-room, and went on board the St. Malo boat shortly after eleven o'clock.

It was very dark. As we stood on the deck, disregarding the drizzle, and with no one near (apparently the whole number of passengers was seven, besides ourselves), a burly figure passed by with the gruff remark, " We are in for a dirty night." It was the captain, and that was all he said ; but to this day I think of that night as simply terrible. I had never been at sea before. As I lay wedged up in the berth of a deck-cabin thoughtfully provided

for me, not so much frightened as bewildered
by the noise of the wind and the shocks of the
heavy seas falling on board, I doubted whether,
even to see my family, could I face such an
experience again.

I have a faint notion that I thought then
that a Channel crossing was always something
like that. I could not have foreseen that before
returning to England I would get on terms
with the sea in a five-ton cutter, and be com-
plimented on my good steering.

Normally we were due at St. Malo at seven
in the morning, but it was three o'clock before
we got ashore and went to the nearest hotel.
Of course, the table d'hôte *déjeuner* was over a
long time ago, and the dining-room was a mere
barren wilderness.

No doubt we could have had something to
eat, but somehow my new husband did not
think of asking for it, and I, not yet accustomed
to my new status of wife, did not like to say
anything, and so we went for a walk in the
streets. Everything was strange, interesting,
and amusing, and about half-past four we
walked into a café to have some tea. They
brought it to us—a teapot, a thing like a bottle
of scent, with *fleur d'oranger* in it, and four hard
biscuits. Then I broke out. My fortitude
gave way. I declared I was dying for some-

thing serious to eat. I reminded him that I had had nothing to eat since dinner the day before. I didn't burst into tears, however.

I had never seen anybody so remorseful. He made as if to rush out of the café—I don't know why, perhaps to raid a provision shop. But as I did not want to be left alone there, I assured him hastily that I could manage to wait till six o'clock, the dinner hour at our hotel. It was my first dinner abroad.

Next morning we started by train to explore Brittany, mainly with a view of finding a small house somewhere on the coast, where we could settle down. It was all very vague.

That evening we arrived in Lannion, and went to the principal inn. There I had my second continental dinner. The table was long and narrow. There were twenty or more people round it, I believe all men, that evening. Some were passing travellers, others belonged to the town and were boarding there. They talked all together, with what seemed to me extraordinary animation. The variety of faces interested me greatly. It could never have occurred to me that one of them, a young man with closely cropped head and a fine thin face, was a poet, M. le Goffic, then quite unknown. Another young man, very pleasant-faced and in a pince-nez, is now a distinguished engineer.

He had come to Lannion to do his first piece of work, which was to electrify the town (Lannion went straight from oil lamps to electric light). What made him interesting was that while engaged in that work he had found time to fall in love with the daughter of a prominent and rather wealthy citizen of the town. After a very few days he confided to my husband, as a safe and sympathetic person, that the course of this affair was not running smoothly. There were complications of all kinds, but from what I was told I received the impression that the young lady was very determined, and I assured Conrad that all would be well, and I was right. Shortly after our return to England, we heard of a happy ending.

Conrad and I then took up our quarters at this very provincial hotel in Lannion, and went out for many drives, looking vaguely for a house which had to be very small and very retired and very cheap. Incidentally we saw some ruins, some bits of Breton landscape, and quite a lot of Breton population. I looked at them with the greatest interest.

Very many young girls were quite pretty, with a spiritual delicacy of feature which seemed to me very surprising in a peasant population. I liked the women's dresses, and at that time many old men were yet to be seen in Breton costume, with long grey locks flowing from under their round hats. Their thin faces had a sort of refined dignity, and I enjoyed immensely the novelty of all this. Our guide and friend was our driver, a round-faced man of forty, from whom we hired the carriage. He was a widower with a lot of small children and he was an excellent father. Conrad told me that he was a hater of priests and, in that land of Catholic Faith, a determined atheist. It's a fact that he never took off his hat when passing a church, but he was a kindly man and scrupulously honest in his charges. One day he told us that he had heard of a good peasant house just built. Nobody had lived in it yet. And when we heard that it was on Ile Grande, we thought it would probably be retired enough. Ile Grande is just a big piece of rock with a very broken-up surface and a few patches of thin grass which the inhabitants call fields. I don't think there was a single tree on it. All the population lived in a small cluster of houses.

The house of which Prijean spoke was certainly new, built of rough stone, and for a peasant's house was rather sumptuous. It was also very clean. There was a large kitchen with a big fireplace, and with beds like ship's berths along the walls, but fitted with doors like cupboards. Of course we did not use them.

There were two rooms upstairs, and in them we found beds of the usual kind. Looking towards the setting sun, there was nothing between that house and North America but the whole sweep of the Atlantic Ocean, and on stormy days the salt spray flew right into the great stone quarry where some stone-cutters worked every day. We could just hear the metallic ring of their tools. I looked at all this wild strangeness with a little awe, but certainly with plenty of hope.

The house was furnished with just mere necessaries. We took our meals in a little room partitioned off the kitchen, off an oilcloth, but we had napkins. This is characteristically French. The bed sheets were unbleached coarse linen, made up of two widths, with a seam in the middle that in its rigidity and harshness reminded one of the long stone walls dividing the so-called fields. All the glass was greenish. The crockery was thick and heavy. It was indeed the simplest life—but who wanted more ? There is no doubt in my mind that it was a happy time. From a certain point of view it was momentous also. But that I did not know. And yet it was Ile Grande which saw the beginning of " The Nigger of the *Narcissus* " and also of " The Rescue ! "—the novel that was published the

year before our silver wedding anniversary !
I entered now upon my duties of a literary
man's wife (the duties of the early days, at
any rate). My instrument was a strange little
typewriter called the Marriott. It had a
sliding bar containing the type, and was worked
with a striker. You had to slide the bar about
and stamp the letter by pressing the striker.
In its primitive character that machine matched
the peasant's cottage perfectly, but you had to
be extremely careful how you moved that bar,
because if you went ever so little too far, all
the type would fall on the floor. At first, I
remember spending quite a lot of time on
my knees, picking up the letters. Yet a lot of
that first tentative text got copied into type
somehow. The end of each page was a small
triumph. It was a happy time.

The climax of a long-drawn excitement
came with the arrival of a four-ton cutter with
a very pretty name, *La Pervenche*. Conrad
had hired her from a retired shipmaster with
whom he struck an acquaintance in Lannion.
He was a tall, fat man, with a very big face,
slightly grizzled hair, and blue eyes. There was
also Madame Lebras, short, fair, and by no means
thin ; and a lot of little Lebras. All those
people could not have taken a greater interest
in our fortunes if they had known us for years.

So one day Captain Lebras sailed *La Pervenche* round, and turned up at our cottage for *déjeuner*, having left the boat anchored on the stretch of sands between Ile Grande and the mainland. That *déjeuner* would have been bolted if it had not been for Captain Lebras, who took his time over the omelette and the sausages, his fromage and his café. But at last we dragged him away to the shore, and then walked over the uncovered sands for quite a mile and stood at last in the shadow of the *Pervenche*. On the coast of Brittany the ebbing tide leaves an immense extent of glistening sands on which the uncovered rocks and islands stand up like buildings and monuments of some immense ruined town. Later, we often used to walk out to our cutter—which had two wooden supports to keep her upright—just after the tide had turned, clamber on board by means of a ladder, pull it up after us, and sit in the cockpit till she floated, when we started for a sail for four or five hours, or perhaps for a three or four days' cruise along the coast.

It was in the *Pervenche* that I graduated as a fore-and-aft helmsman (good) and a look-out (first-class). My eyesight was always very good, and some of those pinnacles of rocks just awash at high water wanted some looking out for. Sometimes we would go to Lannion (our town) by sea, round the coast, and up the river.

On such occasions the public rumour that "les Anglais" from Ile Grande had arrived would spread rapidly, and in an incredibly short time Captain Lebras, his wife, and some of his children would appear on the quay and give us a public reception. On certain days there would be a crowd, too, because the quay bordered the market-place. Presently we would get a private reception in the hotel from the proprietor, Mr. Lhomais, a little man so completely round that he resembled an enormous and extended ball, and by the two young Breton girls who managed the hotel for him (he was a widower), running all day long, up and down, in and out, never at rest, and always smiling. Those two girls first gave me an idea how French women could, and would, work. It would have seemed cruel, if they had not been so cheerful about it. It was a pleasant change to spend a couple of days in Lannion. We would dine at the table d'hôte, see some new faces, a few familiar ones, hear the latest news of Mr. de Fage's love affair, and put in time watching from our bedroom windows the humours of the town. On market-days I used to sit there as if in a box in a theatre, looking on at the frank comedy of the market-place.

3

The market was mostly a pig-market.   It was rich in most laughable incidents, verging on knockabout farce, with now and then the tragic, despairing note of a squealing pig.   It was most fascinating.   I must also explain that it was the only show one could get in that town.

When the time came for returning to our island, we would walk to the boat escorted by the Lebras couple and some of the children. Madame Lebras's speeches to me sounded most affectionate always ; but I could only answer them by nods and smiles, though I also had quite a liking for her.   On one occasion, after I had been helped into the boat and was sitting ready at the tiller, I observed that Madame Lebras had detained my husband on the quay. She talked to him earnestly, clasping her hands and glancing in my direction, while he seemed amused.   After we got away down the river a little, I asked him what it was she had talked to him about.   I had an idea that it was about me.   Conrad confirmed it.   " She talked very nicely," he said, " and what she wanted to impress me with most was that ' *Madame Conrad est une ange !* ' if you want to know."   This silenced me.   What more could I have hoped for ?   I don't think I ever had such a compliment paid to me again, or if I had, Conrad forgot to tell me of it.

It was on our return from one of those trips that I felt for the first time the sense of heavy responsibility when Conrad had a violent attack of gout. Nobody on Ile Grande could understand a word I said; indeed, most of the older people did not know a word of French. Our doctor, a retired naval surgeon, with a red ribbon in his buttonhole, a dear old man, came every day from the mainland, but even he could only understand and speak very few words of English. For a whole long week the fever ran high, and for most of the time Conrad was delirious. To see him lying in the white canopied bed, dark-faced, with gleaming teeth and shining eyes, was sufficiently alarming, but to hear him muttering to himself in a strange tongue (he must have been speaking Polish), to be unable to penetrate the clouded mind or catch one intelligible word, was for a young, inexperienced girl truly awful. I watched him night after night, powerless to do anything except to give him something to drink when he wanted it; and for the rest, writing letters by the light of a single candle, pages and pages of them, which in the end I always destroyed in the course of the next day. Everybody seemed too far away to be worried by those outpourings. The sense of there being nobody at hand to help overpowered and silenced me. At last that anxious time came to an end, and we gradually resumed our life as before, though perhaps somewhat less light-heartedly.

Soon after this a large box containing clothes, books, and other articles was forwarded to us from England. I found amongst its contents Conrad's first two manuscripts. Somehow it seemed to me that I had acquired the beginning of a family. " Almayer's Folly " was finished some months before we knew each other, and my printed copy of that book is inscribed to " Miss Jessie George " ; but " An Outcast of the Islands " begins the series of first editions bearing on their first page the simple line, " Dear Jessie's Copy." He never would talk about and still less show his work to any one. Those words, however, only written before I had come to take up my part in his work, treating of many skies, of distant places, and strange events, seemed to me impregnated with the essence of his past life, of which after all I knew then so very little, and understood perhaps even less. He himself seemed to think those pages mere food for the wastepaper basket, but they became the object of my anxious though secret care. All through my married life I tried to protect the manuscripts against the consequences of his contemptuous indifference. A certain yellow chest of drawers became their refuge for many years, till most of them went to America and met, lately, their rather blatant auction-room fate.

Cruising in the *Pervenche* was our one form of relaxation. We sailed her in fair weather, and sometimes in weather which for me, at any rate, was quite bad enough to long for some sheltered anchorage. For crew, Conrad engaged a pensioned old seaman, a native of Ile Grande. It is pleasant to think that, notwithstanding our impecunious state, we have been as good as a gold-mine to one human being at least. French naval pensions are very small, and his relations, with whom he lived, considered our Milaud rather in the light of a charge. He couldn't do much, but they made him look after the cow. During his first interview with Conrad, he said, with an air of intense disgust, " *Je soigne la vache—que voulez-vous ?* " He was not exactly likeable. He was often grumpy. The dark secret of his life consisted in his being blind in one eye. He kept it from us admirably, and he looked sorry when, after having been paid for the last time, he said good-bye, and went back to *soigner la vache*—disgusting occupation—to the end of his days.

But between the cruises some good work was done. Directly after his bad attack of gout, still weak and very shaky, Conrad began and finished the short story, "An Outpost of Progress." During the three weeks or so it took him to do this, his humour was sardonic. Then he wrote "The Idiots." Much of our Ile Grande life is in that short story, for which Conrad had, I think, an unreasonable contempt. The stone-cutters are in it, our landlady is in it, and the feeling of our surroundings, perhaps a little more sombre than the reality. We saw the actual idiots while being driven by our friend, Prijean, from Lannion to Ile Grande. I won't describe the idiots. Conrad has done that ; but the story had its origin in Prijean's remark just after we had passed them sprawling in the ditch. " Four—hein. And all in the same family. That's a little too much. And the priests say it's God's will!" In addition to these two stories Conrad wrote certainly two chapters of " The Nigger of the *Narcissus*," and a good many pages of what may be called the introduction to " The Rescue " —pages that were to precede the beginning of the dramatic action. Very, very little of all that is left in the published book, but I can catch here and there, in a phrase or paragraph, the precious feeling of those early days. They slipped by quickly. He wrote ; I typed ; and when we didn't go out for a sail we took long walks along the shore over uncovered sands and bare rocks, always with one eye on the watch for the return of the tide. We exchanged greetings with seaweed gatherers, and often walked back with them in the rear of the slow-moving carts.

And then we had a visitor. He appeared at our door unheralded. He was a man on a walking tour in Brittany, who had heard tales of the English people at Ile Grande, and whom curiosity had induced to step out of his way along the coast to see what all the talk amounted to. I don't know whether he was disappointed, but I suspect strongly he didn't know what to make of us. He might have been thirty-five or so, and a senior bank-clerk on his holiday. He was a most pleasant man, who, whatever his impressions may have been, concealed them under a flow of easy talk. We gave him some tea and bread and butter, which he appreciated, and then walked with him to the point on the shore where he struck off straight over the sands—for he disdained to use the causeway. When half-way across he stopped to wave his hand to us. We waved our hands too, and turned back towards our cottage. That sympathetic fellowship of thought and feeling which grows with married years was already established between us, yet I believe that at that moment of parting with a stranger, we both felt a slight touch of loneliness. It was a September day and dusk was falling round us. That evening I hinted at my wish to get back and find a permanent home. I do not think that Conrad felt the same need, but he agreed at once. A conviction of the significance of his work had begun to grow upon me—I mean of its significance to himself, of which he did not seem to be then so aware as he might have been. I felt that his work would be not only the best but the absolutely necessary thing for him—for that deeper self-realisation of which he never spoke and sometimes seemed to think too lightly. Of course I was ready for anything, but I made the best of the momentary mood provoked by the solitary figure of our visitor waving to us a farewell from the sands. It was a sound inspiration, and Conrad was perfectly reasonable. In less than a week's time we embarked at St. Malo for Southampton. The delightful night of that return passage, starry and calm and friendly, I spent on deck in a comfortable hooded chair. I opened my eyes, to see my native land, represented by the Isle of Wight, looking extremely attractive at daybreak. Our early days were over.

III

THE EARLY YEARS

THE early years of our joint history began in Essex in a charming farmhouse which I have been told was Carolinian. Of that I am no judge. It had a low body and two short wings with high gables, and it was built of lath and plaster. Its name was Ivy Walls. Its greatest attraction consisted in its nearness to the village of Stanford, where Mr. and Mrs. G. F. W. Hope were then living. They were Conrad's oldest English friends. Theirs had been the first English home that had been opened to him. I remember, shortly after we were engaged, his telling me that now his uncle was dead, Mr. and Mrs. Hope, as far as feelings could go, were the nearest relations he had in the world, and that he wanted to take me to make their acquaintance. I knew the extent of the friendship and gratitude he felt for them, and I knew that they would be kindly disposed towards me ; but on the occasion of that first visit I was feeling so painfully shy that even Mrs. Hope's most friendly reception could not put me at my ease for some time. I shall never forget the great assistance I received from the youngest child of the house, then a boy of five, who, prompted by the miraculous instinct of children, kept me in countenance by coming to my side and ultimately letting me take him up on my knee. I managed to become more like myself long before we left in the evening ; and I should have been an ungrateful wretch if I had failed to respond to the atmosphere of quiet and sincere goodwill which I felt around me from the very first moment of arrival. A couple of days later Conrad told me that just as we were going away, while I was being helped with my wraps, Mrs. Hope took him aside to whisper her approval of his choice and to predict confidently the success of our matrimonial venture. Without pretending to be unduly mistrustful of myself, I will confess that I was greatly cheered and comforted by this proof of having made a good impression. No wonder, then, that we both wished to begin our home life near such valued and trusted friends.

It was while awaiting the arrival of our eldest boy that Conrad finished " The Nigger of the *Narcissus.*" The writing was done by the end

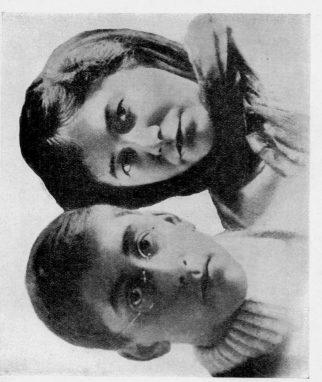

ALFRED BORYS KONRAD KORZENIOWSKI
AND HIS MOTHER IN 1914

of November, and a couple of days afterwards I finished typing it—still with the Marriott. This was the last piece of work done on that machine. It was retired on the upper shelf of a cupboard and forgotten when we moved— most ungrateful treatment. It was succeeded by a mighty Yost.

Our boy Borys was born in January 1898, on a mild and bright forenoon, while Conrad (so I have been told) was wandering vaguely among the beds of the kitchen garden. Suddenly he heard a child cry, and approaching the house where Rose, the maid we had then, was at work—" Send that child away at once; it will disturb Mrs. Conrad ! " he shouted.

" It's your own child, sir," the girl answered indignantly.

Just then my mother ran downstairs to give him a few details, " Such a big boy," and ran back indoors. Whatever his feelings might have been, he managed to conceal them beneath an air of detached interest.

A few days afterwards came a letter from Mr. Heinemann, to say that W. H. Henley had definitely accepted the " Nigger " for a serial. As I knew what importance Conrad attached to being published in the *New Review*, I was made perfectly happy by the news. He immediately went on with " Karain," a story which he had begun in the previous December. A few weeks afterwards that tale was accepted by Mr. William Blackwood for his magazine, which Conrad also regarded as a piece of luck. All this added to my feeling of contentment and peace. The baby, too, was a very peaceful person. He cried just enough for the good of his lungs, and only once disgraced himself by screaming most horribly at Mr. Edward Garnett with such fear and apparent dislike that it took us all aback. We were extremely mortified, but Edward Garnett displayed a benevolent indulgence. " It's probably my spectacles," he said.

When Borys was five weeks old, he paid his first visit to a country house. We spent ten days with Stephen Crane and his wife in Ravenbrook.

Edward Garnett and John Galsworthy were two friends of Conrad's bachelor-days, but they accepted me without question, as though I had been part of Conrad's appointed fate, engaging his thoughts and care like the ships he had sailed, like the books he wrote. One of the most satisfactory memories of the past is that all his friends accepted me on indisputable terms. Though I have not many illusions about my merits I must say that I never had the slightest doubt about the sincerity of their feelings towards me. I may truly say that I was never made to feel that I was "in the way," and this, I take it, was a great compliment. As to Conrad himself, his view was characteristically conscientious and simple. I remember him once telling me that almost directly after we were married (perhaps within two hours) he perceived what he had done, and got into a panic at the thought that he didn't know what it was to live with a woman. He hadn't the slightest notion how to take care of a young girl — a wife — not even from observation. What chance had he had of learning about married life ? Not at school and still less on the high seas, while his days ashore were intervals of utter loneliness. It was only natural, he said, that he should have been frightened. But he perceived very soon that the young girl, now his wife, could not only take care of herself but also knew how to take care of him ; and then he understood the blessedness of the married state. On another occasion, in the course of discussing a person we knew, he declared that he couldn't "see himself" married to anybody else—he couldn't even begin to imagine such a thing. It was perfectly ridiculous. That, too, was a great compliment. With the arrival of the first child a subtle change came upon our intimate feelings, a new sense of the enclosed and simple unity of our lives.

We never managed to beat the record of three
such auspicious events in about two months.
Our first home in Ivy Walls is memorable
mainly on that account, and for my first meeting with Mr. Cunninghame Graham. We didn't
live there very long. Its low situation, practically on the Essex Marsh, was a serious draw-
back. We decided, with great reluctance, for
it meant leaving the Hopes, to move into a
farmhouse, in Kent, rented to us by Mr. F. M.
Hueffer, whose acquaintance we had lately made.
The idea was that we should stay there six
months and look about us ; but in the end we
took it over completely, and we did not leave
it till our eldest boy was ten years old.

Every mother knows the intense delight of
having the care of a tiny child—the proud
delight of knowing that you are everything
in the world to that small mortal, and that
without *you* for him the sun could never shine.
The most devoted of fathers count for much
less for the first few years. This is one of
the arrangements made by Providence which
mothers understand and approve. At any
rate, I approved of it ; I even thought it beautiful. There were anxious days, of course, but
on the whole the three first years of our boy's
life were the freest from all anxiety.

I can truly say that I enjoyed every moment

of both our boys' early childhood. Neither of them ever had a nurse, but we had a maid who was greatly attached to them, who came to us very young and remained for twenty years.

Pent Farm, though charmingly situated, was rather lonely, and we had some difficulty in getting girls to stay. Mr. John Galsworthy, to whose unfailing friendship we both owe more than can be expressed in words, who used to run down often for a day or two days' visit, had many glimpses of me in the kitchen (it opened straight from the dining-room), with Borys on one arm, while my other hand hovered over the saucepans from which the next meal would come. In fact, he and other guests used often to walk right in and greet me there on their arrival.

The early years, the home of which was Pent Farm, fell into two periods—the first one of four years, marked by Conrad's better health, he always referred to as his " Blackwood " period. While the boy learned to walk and talk and take his place in the world, Conrad wrote " Youth " and " The Heart of Darkness " —stories that attracted attention. He then turned to " Lord Jim," of which I think about fifteen pages had been written in Ivy Walls. Into this period also fall the two collaborated novels with Mr. F. M. Hueffer, who was a very frequent visitor, staying with us sometimes for many days, while we used to drive often over to Winchelsea, where the Hueffers had a charming bungalow. We had rooms in an hotel, but we generally spent our days with them.

It was at that time that I saw Mr. Henry James for the first time. Conrad knew him before, but he came over from Rye to call on us and make my acquaintance. Our small boy, a very important person now (though the fact was concealed from him as much as possible), earned the esteem of his father on that occasion. He hated to be nursed by strangers. Mr. Henry James at once took him on his knee and forgot his existence, now and then giving him an absent-minded squeeze while talking to Conrad. We expected a petulant protest and a determined wriggle to get away, but the child's tact, his instinctive sense of Henry James's personality, surpassed our highest expectations. He sat perfectly resigned and still for more than half an hour, till Mr. Henry James released him with a kiss. Conrad's opinion of his son's character went up considerably from that day. The boy's first remark when he saw Mr. James cross the street was, " Oh, Mama dear, isn't he an elegant fowl ? " I had been reading Lear's *Book of Nonsense* to him.

It was during our occupation of Pent Farm, in that first most care-free period, that I received my due tribute of having a book dedicated to me. I did not think that it was over-due, but I was beginning to wonder when it would come. It came in the volume of stories called " Youth " which followed " Lord Jim," though the first two stories in it were written before that long novel. The inscription consists merely of the words, " To my Wife," but the motto on the title-page arrested my attention. I knew that Conrad's title-page quotations had always a close and direct relation to the contents of the book itself, and that they often expressed the mood in which the work was written. After having pondered a little over this one, I decided to ask him whether that quotation from *Grimm's Tales* had been selected in reference to the book, for indeed I was puzzled a little by it. He said, no—not to the text, but to the dedication alone. It runs like this : " But the dwarf said, ' No ; something human is dearer to me than the wealth of all the earth.' "

Later, much later, the literary critics seemed to find that the end of the Blackwood period marked a change in Conrad's manner. My attitude towards his work was never critical (they were too much part of himself) ; if

4

anything, it was maternal. I welcomed them
with affection more than with any other
feeling ; with curiosity, too, for now they were
typewritten in London, and Conrad, without
being secretive, disliked extremely letting anybody see unfinished work. His references to
it were of the briefest kind. But if he was
evolving a new manner, then the volume called
" Typhoon," standing as it does between the
end of the Blackwood phase and the beginning
of a phase marked by " Nostromo," may be
regarded as a transition book. Those tales
were noticed in a particular way ; in a sort
of way which induced Mr. Harvey, afterwards
Ambassador to England but then the editor of
Harper's Magazine, to buy " Nostromo " for
his firm without seeing it, and, in fact, quite a
long time before the book was finished. While
working at it, Conrad had a serious illness which
caused much anxiety to me and to his friends.
He recovered surprisingly quickly, and we went
for a change to London. There he managed to
do some work, actually in lodgings (to my great
surprise) and under very adverse circumstances.
For it was then that I first became a source
of anxiety to him.

The trouble was sprung on him one frosty
morning when he had gone out early to breakfast with Mr. John Galsworthy. I on my

side had gone out to do some early shopping.
On coming out from Barker's I slipped the
cartilage of both knees at once and fell on
the pavement, hurting very badly the knee
already damaged by an accident I had at the
age of sixteen. I had with me my maid and
the small boy. Two passers-by helped me to
my feet, and I managed to walk into a café
some yards distant and send a message to
Conrad. He came in a great fright and helped
me to walk to our lodgings in Gordon Place.
My fortitude then failed me, and it was many
days before I could move off the couch. On
that day, which opened like any other, twenty
years ago as I write these words, the whole
colouring, the mental complexion, and even
the details of our future life, became per-
manently affected before half-past ten in the
morning !

At times, looking back on it, it seems a little
nightmarish. Before " Nostromo " was finished
an operation had been decided upon, and when
the book appeared I was in a nursing-home for
that purpose. It was my first separation from
husband and child, though they were not very
far away—in a flat in Addison Road. The day
they both escorted me to the nursing-home
and left me there, I was preternaturally wide
awake, and yet as if frozen inside. I remember

being amused at the masculinity of the small boy (aged six and a half), who was determined to cut short the emotional situation. He just gave me a hug and two kisses, and then marched out of the room on to the landing without looking back. The last thing I remember of Conrad, in the gloom of that room, was the gleam of his teeth shown in a sort of nervous society smile which he bestowed on me from the doorway. My next half-hour all alone, just before I was put into bed for many months, was rather awful. I have had since plenty of opportunities to get used to nursing-homes and operations.

The next event which followed was our journey to Italy. My second journey to the Continent was performed like a bale of goods— very valuable goods indeed, which had to be carried with immense precautions from train to steamer, and from steamer to train, and had to have a whole sleeping-compartment on the train to itself. The return journey, some five months afterwards, was done under less humiliating conditions; I was glad when we resumed our old life at Pent Farm.

But it was not the same. Walking, as it is understood by the hale and sound part o mankind, was out of the question for me; and yet I could move and I did move, not exactly like a cripple but with difficulty, as though dragging an invisible weight riveted to my leg. I took up my directive part in the home life, but everything seemed a little more difficult than before. " Nostromo " had turned out a black frost as far as the public went. Conrad was bitterly disappointed. This was the only time I saw him display any feeling about the fate of his books. And I didn't wonder at it, because I knew how much effort, what an amount of vitality and nervous force, he had expended in writing that book. For some time he could not recapture the creative mood, except for a story or two ; but he found refuge from that distress in writing the marvellous pages (so I think them) of " The Mirror of the Sea."

Our Pent Farm period comes practically to an end with the advent of John, our second boy, though he was not a native of the place. Mr. and Mrs. John Galsworthy lent him their house in London to begin life in. While we were awaiting his arrival there, Conrad was finishing the first and shorter version of " The Secret Agent." As I did not know in the least what the book was about, I could not account to myself for the grimly ironic expression I used often to catch on his face, whenever he came to give me a look-in. Could it have reference to the expected baby ? No ! it was only a reflection of the tone of the book's. Conrad was as pleased with this baby as with the other boy. His first remark, I believe, was, " That fellow looks like an Italian." Later it was amusing to me to watch John, aged about three, winding his father round his little finger.

Our early years had their own joys and sorrows.

IV

LATER DAYS

THE end of our early years was over-shadowed by cruel anxiety, as we nearly lost both our boys at the same time—the baby from sheer exhaustion during severe and prolonged whooping-cough, and the elder, then approaching his tenth year, from pleurisy. And we were in an hotel in Champel, near Geneva, at the time! I flatter myself that I saved John's life after the doctor had given him up, by the expedient of feeding him out of a spoon. He was a most pitiable object, not to be looked at without tears, and he simply had not the strength to help himself ; but he was still able to swallow. His recovery was marvellous in its rapidity and completeness. While I was fighting for the last spark of life in John, Conrad looked after Borys and earned my additional respect by managing, under those circumstances, to rewrite and expand by some 15,000 words the end of " The Secret Agent."

That book in its present form marks for me literally the end of our early days. After bringing thankfully both children home we decided to leave Pent Farm and Kent. We moved to a house called Someries, in Bedfordshire. I conclude we must have been suffering from temporary aberration of mind, because we immediately discovered that the only place for us, after all, was the county of Kent. In Bedfordshire we felt as if we had been exiled. Our tenancy of Someries did not last more than a year and a half. Conrad, without suffering from any acute attacks of gout, was being mildly tormented by it all the time. Most of the stories in the " Set of Six " were written there, and almost all the whole first part of the novel called " Under Western Eyes "—the only book which, from a few words which he dropped at different times, I think he regretted having begun at all. He told me once that this work, which he considered to be intensely personal in its views and its style, would inevitably be pronounced by critics to be derivative. " They will be trying to drag in comparisons with Russian writers of a certain kind," he said. The mere thought of that was odious to him, and I quite understood why : he held tenaciously to Poland's Western temperament, traditions and culture being altogether removed from Slavism, except geographically. His apprehensions about the critics were realised to some extent—to my great regret.

Otherwise Someries is memorable to me through the fact that the first number of *The English Review* was partly edited and actually put together there ; that final operation took the whole of one night. Mr. F. M. Hueffer arrived late in the afternoon, accompanied by his secretary and his sub-editor, all carrying parcels of papers and very little other luggage. Each took possession of a separate room, and that night nobody slept a wink except the baby and the servants. I went to bed in the usual way, only to listen all night to the sounds of footsteps and voices conversing between the ground floor and the first floor over the banisters. The consumption of lamp oil and candles was prodigious. But I like to remember that period of excitement, if only for the reason that one of Conrad's most precious books, the " Personal Record," owes its existence to *The English Review*.

From spacious Someries we changed into a cottage of six tiny rooms. But we were back in Kent. Those were straitened quarters, but we made up our minds to remain in them for years if need be, waiting till we could discover something more adequate. In a room not much bigger than a monk's cell, but much more encumbered with furniture, Conrad finished " Under Western Eyes " ; and it was in that same room (as the most cheerful of them) that he lay through nearly three months of a most severe illness, during which he says that he never came to himself or opened his eyes either night or day without seeing me by his bedside.

I knew from the first what it would be, and had a couch put in there for myself. I could have depended on but little aid from an old maid who helped me to look after John. Our cottage neighbours were very kind and sympathetic to us strangers, and we had the unremitting friendly care of our doctor—the same one who used to attend us in our Pent Farm days.

It was four months before I took Conrad for his first convalescent drive. " Under Western Eyes " had been out more than a month, and had, practically, no sale whatever. It was unfortunate, yet Conrad did not seem to care, and we seemed condemned for life to that six-roomed cottage, which had grown odious to both of us. But on that day our luck changed. As we drove along a familiar lane we passed a house we had known by sight for years. It had the appearance of being unoccupied ; the gate of the drive was open. I was prompted to direct the driver to turn into it ; the rustic caretaker thought there was no harm in us seeing it.

Conrad was much too weak to walk about, but he sat on the low window-sill of the room that was afterwards our dining-room, while I went all over the house. It was not big, though after the cottage it seemed palatial, and John found a great delight in shouting in the empty rooms. Conrad and I felt we must have this house.

The caretaker, pocketing my half-crown, assured us that it was impossible, as the owner was going to make a week-end cottage of it for himself. Still, the caretaker gave us his name and his London address. To make a long story short, with a rapidity that seemed like enchantment but was really the magic of human kindness, the house became ours on a yearly tenancy. I sent Conrad away to the care of a friend while I directed the move (only seven miles), and put every bit of furniture in its place according to a plan which I had already in my mind's eye. Then I wired to him to come home. As I watched him come along the platform of the railway station I thought how ghostlike he still looked. Next day after breakfast he walked, still shaky, into the room

which combined the functions of drawing-room
and study, and wrote there the first pages of
" The Smile of Fortune."

That auspicious title ushered in a period of
happy activity and comparatively good health
for him. Our eldest boy, to his great joy,
entered the cadet training-ship *Worcester*, a
'74 very much of Nelson's ships' type, the
captain of which was Sir David Wilson Barker,
a very distinguished scientific merchant-sea-
man. The headmaster, Mr. A. Beattie, was
also a man of exceptional ability, much beloved
by the generations of young seamen who passed
through his hands. It was delightful to think
that the boy was doing well and was perfectly
happy there. John, too, was happy, leading an
outdoor life. For my part, I confess that I was
conscious that the state of my operated knee
was growing more unsatisfactory. I was very
seldom completely free from some pain, but I
said nothing about it, hoping always for a turn
for the better and watching with delight the
progress of the children and the birth of the
books. " 'Twixt Land and Sea," " Within the
Tides," the novels " Chance " (the first library
success) and " Victory " (the last of the pre-
war works), were written here. " Victory " was
only named after it was finished. Conrad had
given himself up to this work with great

intensity, but, as usual, without talking about it.

Before the war-shadow fell on our thoughts and on the very spirit of the land, our eldest boy left the *Worcester* with a good leaving certificate. We had been invited to a Polish country-house, and Conrad was very glad that the boys should see something of the Polish life and visit Cracow, the town of his own schooldays, before they grew too old to care for the early associations of their father's life.

Conrad's impressions and feelings on that journey have been related by him in three articles called " Poland Revisited," and now I shall record mine.

V

OUR VISIT TO POLAND IN 1914

IN Joseph Conrad's account of this journey, he says it was my wish that we should take the unusual route across the North Sea. It was, as a matter of fact, his suggestion. I welcomed it because it seemed to make the journey more of an adventure. An adventure it certainly was to me, since I was to see my husband's native country for the first time, and in company with our two boys ; let alone its being the first time for many years that Conrad himself had set foot there. He used to say he had not been to Poland for forty years—presumably he had forgotten his last two visits : the first, when he was writing " Almayer's Folly," some of which was actually written in his uncle's house ; and the second, after the death of that uncle in '83 or '84. I have been often sorry that he would never fix some dates by reference to old letters or papers. I tried many times to persuade him to let me

write them up.   It would have saved no little
confusion.

There was always, in the case of all our pro-
jected trips, so great an atmosphere of un-
certainty round them, so big a " perhaps," that
I hardly believed we were actually going, even
when the passports arrived.   As it turned out,
even then nothing was really decided.   He had
forgotten some important formality as to the
date of his nationalisation, and he had omitted
to put his full name, Korzeniowski.   These
omissions delayed matters.   The proper passport only reached us finally the day before we
were due to start.   Our friends awaiting us in
London, for we were to be a party of six, had
almost given us up.   However, our papers
arrived, none of the disasters Conrad had pre-
dicted happened, and in due course we left
Capel House to drive to Ashford, the first stage
of our journey.   It was a very, very hot day
towards the end of July.   As far as I could
arrange things I had dressed the small boy,
John, as lightly for travelling as possible.   We
had gone less than a mile on our way when
Conrad turned round in a sudden fury because
the boy was not wearing his leather gaiters.
" Why had I insisted on buying them, if he
wasn't going to wear them ?   Better pitch
them overboard."   All the rest of the journey

to town, those gaiters worried his troubled spirit. Had it not been that I was not quite certain which of the two big trunks contained them, I believe I would have sacrificed the boy's comfort for the sake of peace. However, a real grievance came up when our friends were almost too late for the train. Up and down the platform, in and out of the railway carriage, I had perforce to climb. We couldn't start because our friends had the tickets. At last we were off, tired out completely, and with a feeling of having only just escaped a terrible tragedy. A moment after I heard Conrad laughing heartily at something his companion was telling him. When he saw my collapsed condition in the corner of the carriage, he admonished me severely, declaring that if the first part of the long journey had been so fatiguing we had better turn back at once.

At Harwich I was faced with a formidably long walk over the rails and a long, interminable platform. We were both exhausted by the time we got on board. I was thankful when the small boy and I had reached our cabin. It was an uncomfortable passage. Conrad had impressed upon our fellow-travellers the need for economy. This was always a fatal proceeding with him, because he was never content with cheap accommodation. He would have rushed me out of my quarters and bundled me into others, but by this time I was quite incapable of further effort. I lay between the boards forming the top berth and my own, feeling indifferent to everything—even whether we completed our journey or not. Almost every half-hour I opened my eyes, to see Conrad bending anxiously over me. " What had come to me ? Why had I given in like this ? Such behaviour was enough to rob him of all confidence ; it made him anxious. It was not the thing to spring on a fellow." In vain I assured him that a little rest and quiet was all I needed, and that in the morning I would be ready to move wherever he might want me to go.

The next day we met on deck, everybody looking as if the passage had been somewhat rougher than they quite liked. Our fellow-passengers were mostly Germans. The captain was certainly pro-German, and Conrad took an instant dislike to him. There was a portly German woman, who had accompanied her husband and son from America ; their anxiety to see the first German light struck me as almost pathetic. The good woman sat spread liberally over a small wooden trunk placed exactly over the starboard paddle-wheel. A youngish man, with fierce moustaches waxed to

5

a stiff point, his restless eyes showing under the
peak of his cheese-cutter cap, paced impatiently
to and fro. He had been over to England to
bring his two boys back to Germany from
school. One would almost fancy, in the light
of later events, that he was afraid he would not
get back before war had been declared. The
two boys kept close to their father's heels,
silent and subdued. Now and again I heard
Conrad and our friend discussing the possibility of war, but they did not seem particularly
anxious, and they talked as though such a con-
tingency was not by any means imminent.
We were some time getting ashore in Hamburg ;
there were a lot of horses to land. By this
time the feeling between the captain and Conrad
had become decidedly unpleasant. I was thankful to get away. We stayed a few hours in
Hamburg, visited the Zoo, lunched, and took
our train for Berlin in the afternoon. Arrived
there, we dined. Conrad and the small boy
retired to bed and we other four went to a
music-hall. There was a suppressed excitement in the air which we all remarked upon.
It did not tend to make us feel comfortable.
I don't remember much of what we saw except
some cleverly trained parrots, who talked in
a wonderfully human way. There was also
a company of English dancing-girls. I have

heard since that their hardships were many before they got back to England. The next morning we were decidedly unfortunate. Everything was confusion. We left without any breakfast and nearly missed the train. Being lame I was very slow—and I always tell this in favour of the Hun—the guard of that train held it back two minutes for me. But my smiling thanks he disregarded, and though very voluble, he was not, I fancy, very complimentary ; he ended up by spitting contemptuously on the platform. At the first stopping-place we secured some welcome food—good bread and small, tasty sausages. A bottle of wine cheered us, and the spirit of adventure returned. Four of us played poker, while the small boy and I contented ourselves with counting the telegraph poles and the blue-grey figures, who, armed with a rifle, guarded the numerous little bridges as the train thundered across. Everything looked peaceful, and the country seemed rich and beautiful. We had the carriage to ourselves, and exchanged impressions.

It must have been after six o'clock when the train ran into Cracow. We were all excited, and I could see my husband was deeply moved at being once again in the city where most of his boyhood had been passed. He pointed out several interesting places to us from the carriage window. I rather turned my nose up when we left the station ; the road paving seemed extremely primitive, and the odour of stables and bad draining was somewhat sickening. Conrad noticed my expression. He turned to me rather sharply, remarking, " This is not England, my dear ; don't expect too much."

At the hotel I was touched by the ready friendliness of our reception. Before we had been there half an hour, cards poured in upon us. I saw for the first time what an immense hold one's native country could have upon one. We forgot the possibility of war. Only my husband referred now and then to the ominous fact that troops were even on our first night pouring into the town. He kept saying : " I wonder if it wouldn't be wiser to rush you all home again ? Still, what a fool I would look if nothing came of it after all. What do you think, my dear ? " I cheerfully urged him to be calm and make up his mind to enjoy our visit.

I understood my husband so much better after those months in Poland. So many characteristics that had been strange and unfathomable to me before, took, as it were, their right proportions. I understood that his temperament was that of his countrymen. It was a severe trial to my nerves, those two months amongst strangers—strangers so completely foreign, and all talking in a language of which I knew at most a dozen words. I used to collect all the little Poles I could find and take them to play in our small bedroom. Children have a wonderful way of understanding each other without the need of words.

At night, if I happened to retire early, I would lie anxiously listening to raised voices in the next room, all talking at once. I missed their gestures, which for the most part only showed their utter despair.

The first week after we had arrived passed slowly while we still awaited the *visa* to our passport, which would enable us to fulfil the object of our journey. We had been invited by the mother of our travelling companions to pay a visit to their country-house outside Cracow, just over the Russian frontier. Mrs. Retinger had already gone ahead to help prepare for our coming, while her husband remained with us till our passport should be in order. We took many drives in and round the town, Conrad pointing out to us those places familiar to him during his schooldays. He also told us that Cracow, like our Canterbury, had once had an archbishop murdered in its cathedral. Outside the city was a huge mound of earth that had been carted there by the people in buckets and baskets, and raised as a memorial to their dead. He showed us, too, St. Florian's Gate, through which his father's funeral had passed. I knew already many touching facts about that part of my husband's lonely life. It seemed to draw my own boys closer to me in a curious way. I shall never cease to feel glad that they and I made that memorable journey while, as Conrad said, they were still young enough to feel impressions deeply. After the war there were other mounds, many of them which bore a roughly hewn cross. Once again comedy creeps up close to tragedy. A friend of mine, on seeing a goodly sized mound topped with a cross, remarked sympathetically to a peasant in a tiny village in Poland, " Ah, my friend, I see you too have covered your dead ! " The man scratched his ear reflectively a few moments, and then said in a quiet tone, " They are potatoes, lady."

Next day, at lunch, we noticed an elderly man with a fine white head of hair staring at Conrad with astonishment ; he finally rushed across the room to clasp him in his arms. They fell upon each other's necks, embracing closely. He was one of Conrad's old school friends. That afternoon we paid a visit to his house a few miles out of Cracow. We had his car, which was very comfortable except for the fact that the rain came through a large hole in the roof and ran down our necks. However, it stopped raining before we reached our destination, and we enjoyed our first introduction to a Polish country-house ; from the verandah where we sat we looked over field beyond field of sugar-beet. The big flat fields stretched as far as the eye could reach, and only now and again a team of horses, either harnessed to a farm cart or leisurely drawing a plough, relieved the monotony. Our hostess had received us with gracious hospitality, and very soon I felt as much at home as I could have done if I had known them for years and years. There was such an air of peace and tranquillity everywhere. War—impossible ! But I often caught the word, accompanied by a sorrowful shake of the head. Poland did not anticipate anything good for herself out of a war. Yet, curiously enough, to her has come the greatest change : at last she is a self-governed country again.

While we were at tea, our hostess came quietly into the room and with an anxious expression announced gravely that the soldiers were already taking the horses from the ploughs and carts in the fields. It had come, then, this war in which we had decided not to believe ! During our hurried journey back to Cracow, we saw that horses were being taken from all sorts of conveyances. One group of distressed ladies were left helplessly sitting in their carriage while their fine pair of black horses stepped gracefully down the road in charge of a couple of soldiers. Our friend's car continued its course unmolested, much to our relief. Every turn of the road revealed an officer seated at a little table on some small plot of grass, busy noting the names of owners, while increasing numbers of horses were being led or driven into an enclosure near by. When we reached our hotel, a model of order and decorum a few hours ago, all was bustle and confusion. The manager, a good-looking man, with a fine head of thick black hair, who only that morning had bowed us out of the door, rushed hurriedly forward, his head shaven close, and announced in shrill tones, " I expect to sleep in barracks to-night." In the huge vestibule anxious groups were talking excitedly ; frantic travellers were trying vainly to get at the telephone ; soon appeared, as if from nowhere, fully armed officers and men staggering under enormous bundles of kit. Every one was talking at once. All the small change had mysteriously disappeared ; and it was soon quite evident that it was time for us to make other arrangements. Our fellow-traveller, whose young wife had crossed the

Russian frontier two days before, was endeavouring to hire the hotel car, in the hope of inducing some peasant from the other side to carry a note to tell her to join him at once. Then came the appeal which I had feared. He asked us to allow our eldest boy, Borys, a youth of sixteen, to accompany him. I remember feeling dismay, yet at the same time it was impossible to refuse. We stood at the door watching them enter the car ; my heart rose in my mouth when the manager stepped forward and handed a revolver to each. That was too much for me. I had an instinct that caught : armed, their chance of being shot would be much greater—moreover, I distrusted their prudence. They yielded to my entreaties and returned the revolvers to their owners, who somewhat reluctantly admitted I might be right. The night was horrible. All through the weary hours men poured through the streets, shouting and singing, women cried, and little children lamented miserably. It was not until nearly six in the morning that the car returned. They had found that the Russian guard had left, after blowing up all the bridges, and that the peasants had taken to the woods. Our friend and Borys had spent the night in the Austrian guard-house. Two or more peasants had been heavily bribed to carry the message, but one and all had returned, sheepishly announcing their failure. Borys has told me since how wonderful it all seemed to him, and how that night stands out for him, in spite of the horrors that he was to go through before he reached the age of twenty-one. He remembers an old woman sitting on the steps and rocking herself to and fro, bemoaning that this phantom, War, had already annexed her son ; he remembers the sausages and beer they shared with the guards, and the bitter cold of the hours of waiting.

Two days later we left, having finally decided to seek as a retreat a small health resort in the mountains, a pretty little place called Zakopane. The friendly hotel-manager had not left before our departure ; he managed somehow to hold back the car till he had put me down at the station. Here all was confusion. Nobody knew from where any train was starting, and people were packed so close on the platform that you could not move. We stood together in a bunch, my small boy's coat firmly fastened to mine. At last we were shepherded into a train, hoping fervently that our baggage would by some lucky chance eventually be put in as well. Then began a long, tedious journey upon the mountain rail. At every small station or junction we were drawn on to a siding to let a heavy troop train through. The soldiers' faces seemed to be piled up one on top of the other in the cattle-trucks. All looked hot, thirsty, and exhausted. Girls passed swiftly up and down the train giving them water, and at each level-crossing crowds of women and girls clustered close to the gates weeping bitterly. A terrible sense of disaster reigned everywhere. There was no jaunty pretence of wishing to fight. Perhaps it was some foreboding of the magnitude of the task before them that filled them with so much dismay. How many of those men we saw being conveyed like cattle are alive to-day? We had been fortunate enough to meet a friend, a new friend, who proved most effective in procuring food for us on the way. And it is a curious fact that I really enjoyed the dish of veal and potatoes he handed us through the railway carriage window. Hours passed, and slowly we neared our destination.

The little railway station of Zakopane is engraved for ever on my memory; no photograph or coloured picture could convey the depth of that impression. We soon discovered the dismal fact that only one of our trunks had got through, and, searching through our pockets, we failed to find our registration ticket. The second trunk we recovered in a most unexpected manner two months later in Vienna.

Two days after our arrival we heard that England had come into the war. We had been confident she would. Then followed a nightmare of rumours. During that fortnight we were told that our army had been completely wiped out, and that all our fleet was at the bottom of the sea. Only news from German sources reached us, and every reference to England was accompanied by the most revolting insults. Every cartoon represented England and the English in some odious form. Very few people around us spoke our language, and we understood hardly a word of Polish. Had my husband not retained a perfect recollection of his mother-tongue, our plight would have been terrible indeed. No word could reach us of our relatives or friends in England.

The house where we had found refuge was full of other refugees ; some slept in the dining-room, some in the drawing-room, and one was never out of earshot of excited voices. All talked at once, all were without money, many with scanty clothes. Small change there was none, and the only thing to do was to deposit a hundred-mark note with a café, or shop-keeper, and to spend against it. I had no vest, and when it got very cold I annexed one of Borys's (who had three), and to this day he teases me because I trimmed the neck with a little embroidery as a small concession to my femininity. We had two small bedrooms opening one from the other and on to a narrow wooden verandah. The house was built of enormous logs like a Swiss chalet and surrounded by a small, weedy garden. Numerous fowls of the bantam breed scratched unsuccessfully, and added greatly to its forlorn aspect, besides providing endless cause for trouble between the tenant and the old landlady (of evil aspect), who had retained two rooms on the top floor. There she lived closely shut in with a maid, as ill-conditioned as herself, appearing, as it seemed, always at the worst moments to continue her quarrel with her tenant about the bantams. I discovered that Madame Z. had purchased them from some wily dealer in the fond belief that they would grow into large fowls. It took more than a month to persuade her that they were then at their full size and old at that. Later on a goose with a broken wing was added to the live stock. For two days we bore the sight of the poor bird waddling round, and trying hard to avoid treading on its own wing, which trailed beside it. At last Borys caught it and severed the wing with a small pocket-knife. We dressed the wound with some carbolic on a rag, and the goose became quite friendly. The day it formed the midday meal (an October goose in Poland is as great a traditional feast as our turkey at Christmas), we missed our dinner. Apart from the fact that we were unable to get permission to move from the place, those two months in Zakopane were free from immediate anxiety.

Scarcely an echo of the war reached us. Only trains full of refugees kept pouring in, or native carts with human freight ; clad often in the dress they had been wearing at some dinner-party days before, penniless in spite of valuable jewellery. In one shop window in the main street I have seen hundreds of wedding-rings offered for sale. There were many families, or rather, I should say, parts of large families. One lady had only two of her daughters with her, the other three smaller children and their nurse and governess had been mislaid on the journey. Sometimes the trains remained standing in the station with their passengers still aboard, there not being enough food in the place to admit of more people coming in. Soldiers' uniforms were mostly made by the ladies in the place, and nearly all by hand. Often a young soldier would appear and leave behind him a bundle of wool to be made into socks. There were several small children in our house, and there was one maiden lady of uncertain age who passed her

time, yawning prodigiously, between her meals
in gazing fondly at her tall nephew, a man of
thirty-five or so. She had brought him up
from babyhood, and she had no notion that he
was now a man. He slept in a small bed in her
room, and she handed him his change of clothing
as she must have done for the whole of his life.
He appeared quite normal, except for his stupid
submission to his feminine possessor. I used
to watch him sometimes when there were young
girls in the room, to see if he betrayed any
interest. But beyond a slow smile and a little
extra stroking of his blond moustache he made
no sign.

Madame Z., a charming, highly cultured
woman, was a connection of my husband's by
marriage. She was completely out of her
element here, but very talkative and excitable.
I sometimes went shopping with her in the
village. We would drive the short distance,
do our shopping, and engage another small trap
to return. Almost invariably there would be a
heated argument between her and the driver,
whose eloquence I could not of course understand. It generally ended by the man following her into the house shouting his demands;
if he happened to be fairly old and feeble,
Madame would succeed in ejecting him without
assistance. She would close the door with

great decision, and, before removing her hat, seat herself at the table and begin laying out a patience, grumbling all the time. I had the greatest affection for her and shall treasure her memory always.

Many refugees at Zakopane were subjected to the indignity of having their rooms and luggage searched, while two soldiers with drawn swords remained on the other side of the door. As to ourselves, I have no words to express my appreciation and gratitude for all the kindness that was invariably shown us. We were indeed with friends. One dear old lady and her husband I had a great affection for. Part of their family were at Zakopane, but their son, with his English wife, was in England. When we at last got permission to leave I was able to safely deliver some letters for her in London. One other man who charmed me greatly was the elder brother of General Pilsudski. He had a slight resemblance to the late King Edward, and he possessed a wonderful speaking voice.

About the 6th of October we were able, through the kindness of a Polish military officer, to get permits to proceed to Vienna. The next two days were much occupied, of course, with preparations for departure—preparations which included one large suit-case containing a miniature kitchen : a spirit stove, tins of soup, and other tinned eatables, and a supply of tea, milk, and butter. We also bought a mountaineers' metal box which contained collapsible glasses and convertible knives and forks ; and we would have fared very badly but for our forethought. We left our place of refuge at one in the morning. Snow was lying thick on the ground and frost glistening on the hedges in the moonlight. The two unshod horses and their grisled driver, who was attired in skin shoes made as a continuation of his trousers, and a short skin tunic secured round the waist with a string, made a weird picture in the moonlight. His coarse grey moustache, dripping with moisture, made me shudder. The trap was of the old country-fly type, with two hoods made to meet in the middle, without doors. Underneath was slung a large piece of canvas containing fodder for the two horses ; hung round the back, in what appeared a very unsafe manner, was the luggage. I had never seen so much stowed in such a precarious fashion. I felt quite sure that half would be dropped on the road. The inside of the trap was lined with sheepskins, peopled with tiny creatures which effectively kept us awake. The horses trotted noiselessly along the steep roads. Now and again the driver would dismount and trot by the side, or flick his steeds with a long

6

whip, and allow them to get many yards ahead of him. These moments filled me with dismay. On both sides of the road there was a deep drop, and I remembered hearing, only a few days before, of other travellers on that very road who had been badly hurt by being tipped over the edge while the driver was some distance behind. Every now and then the wheels rumbled over a long wooden bridge, or the driver pulled up with a jerk, while some peasant, who had at last responded to his cries, lifted the long pole fixed across the road. This and the glare of the soldiers' lanterns thrust into our faces, while their owners satisfied themselves we were what our papers stated, were the only incidents till we reached the little wayside station.

We were stiff when we descended from that old rattle-trap. There had been four grown people in it (an influential Polish friend was accompanying us), and the small boy John had lain on our knees. We were all very cold and tired when we reached the station, where seats had been reserved for us in a train for Cracow. The driver landed our luggage, purloined all the straps he could see, and approached me with a flourish. He kissed me on both cheeks before I had a chance to protest ; then, falling on his knees, he pressed the hem of my skirt to his lips. It was the only time during our troubles when I felt like tears. I am afraid I did not appreciate the attention. I glanced down at my dress and my confusion was increased by John's open-eyed astonishment. My husband did not appear to have noticed anything ; by degrees I recovered, and at last I could laugh.

There was only one other occupant of the *coupé* I shared with the two boys—a Grand Duke's chauffeur. Our friend and my husband shared a carriage with a wounded officer and his orderly. The wounded man was grateful for a few sips of hot coffee, which was all he could swallow; but the orderly was famished, and devoured all we could give him. Even at that stage of the war food must have been fairly scarce. When we reached Cracow the guard carefully collected all the small scraps of bread and meat and wrapped them in paper before putting them in his pocket.

I shall never forget the hours we spent in Cracow. We had no permission to leave the station, and had to sit eleven hours on hard wooden chairs. Numerous trains thundered through, stopping to discharge their varied loads of anxious travellers, wounded soldiers, and one or two prisoners. One of these, a tall Russian General, sat stiffly between his two

Austrian captors, glancing superciliously around the big refreshment-room, without taking the least notice of anything going on around him. One of the Austrians, a plump little officer, was exhibiting a bullet hole in his grey-blue cap to a table full of V.A.D. nurses, who were talking excitedly together. We were the only English-speaking people, and we seemed to interest the occupants of the room not a little. I was most sorry for John, who was too young to understand anxiety and too young to take much interest in human nature. I managed at last to make one of the officials understand that I wanted to wash my little boy's hands. The man eyed me up and down and shrugged his shoulders. He then called two very slatternly girls across to him, and gave them some brief directions and the key of the door at the end of the long room. I followed them, with my hand on John's shoulder and leaning on my stick. We passed through long, narrow passages reeking of blood and fennel, past long rows of bloodstained figures seated against the wall, some with their eyes closed; others were evidently trying to endure pain in silence, and sat wringing their hands and swaying slightly to and fro. The railway station was also a dressing-station. Suddenly I caught sight of a huge pail full of human scraps, and

I hurriedly covered my boy's eyes with my hand.

When we got back to the refreshment-room our friend had returned and was imparting some news of moment to my husband. They were speaking Polish, but from their anxious glances in our direction I guessed that the news, whatever it might be, concerned us. The last hour and a half of weary waiting seemed more trying than all the preceding ones. John had exhausted his interest in the little piece of paper, which was all I had to give him, and, poor child, he was very tired. Our train was due to leave at eleven. At last it thundered into the station, and we started on another phase of our too eventful journey. Always at the back of all our minds was the fear that we might be stopped and held up in some remote place away from our Polish friends. Every now and then my husband would ask, " Do you still wish to go on ? " The decision always rested with me, and sometimes, waking at night, I was panic-stricken and almost decided to say so, but with the daylight my courage invariably came back. I held my tongue and we travelled on.

No one had any time to spare for us. Had it not been for our friend, who had made the journey to and from Vienna frequently and

knew the war-time procedure, this stage of
our journey might have been the finish. A
very big man, and somewhat short of breath,
he nevertheless found us a carriage near the
engine, and standing with my husband and
Borys they defended it, while I made my labori-
ous way along the platform, my stick in one
hand and the other on the shoulder of my
youngest boy. I smile now when I think of
that walk. A few paces along the platform
there were drawn up ready to entrain a company of Austrian infantry. The double line
stretched nearly to the end of the long train
where the three figures stood on guard at the
door of our carriage. There was a narrow lane
between the two rows of men, and my native
cheek led me to march right down the middle.
The Austrian officer, his moustaches bristling
with outraged dignity and gesticulating violently,
walked backwards in front of us, protesting
volubly all the way. I had never feared a
soldier in my life, and the fact that these men
were our enemies never entered my head. I
smiled sweetly and continued on my way.
Then followed two long nights and a day in
the cramped quarters of a dirty little railway
carriage. I shared one seat with John, whom I
induced to lie down and sleep, making a pillow
of my lap; the other three huddled themselves

on the opposite seat.   None of us had the heart
to read, and, one and all, we longed for a chance
to take off the clothes we had now been wearing
nearly a week.   Conrad was crippled with a
gouty knee and at the same time worn out with
anxiety.   He perhaps was feeling the discomfort more than any of us.   As for myself, the
bandages I was wearing round my sick knee
had disappeared in the swelling.   Truly we
were all sorry for ourselves, and we had almost
reached a state of indifference to our ultimate
fate.   Our picnic meals were the only break in
the long hours, and still the small boy never
murmured.   I used to try to ease the dreadful
boredom by getting him to count the telegraph
posts and by telling him stories in an under-
tone.   It came to an end at last, and we ran
into the brilliantly lighted station in Vienna.
Then, to our consternation, we discovered that
our other trunk had disappeared.   Fortunately
we had a change of clothes in one of the suit-
cases, but I had been forced to pack them wet.
I did my one and only washing the last day
we were in Zakopane, in the hope of starting
our travels in clean clothes.   Rooms in a very
comfortable hotel had been reserved for us by
our friend, and the garments soon dried when
spread before the fire.   A bath and some supper
and the luxury of a real bed once again seemed

to compensate us for most of our troubles, for that night at least. By the morning the gout had got a firm grip of my husband, and I had no medicine left. As soon as it was light, we went out into the town to seek a chemist who could speak English. One and all had removed the notice from their window, "English spoken here," and we were unsuccessful for some time. At last the expression on the face of one assistant led me to believe that he could perfectly well understand what I said, and I was thankful to find him human enough to give me what I needed, though he carefully refrained from uttering a word. We glanced at many of the shop windows on our way back to the hotel, and we were disturbed to see windows full of maps of England.

The next day we came across an old man, a facsimile of Don Q., immortalised by Captain Kettle, with pointed face, round hat, and the black cloak. This queer individual spoke quite decent English, and undertook to act as guide and interpreter. We started in a taxi to make the round of all the railway stations, trying to recover our lost luggage. Don Q. insisted on sharing my seat in the taxi, and we made the round of the stations with the persistence of despair. At last (so my husband says) I made myself so objectionable to the officials that

they threw open the double doors of a large
kind of shed and gruffly directed us to "look for
ourselves." On the very top of the pile, which
must have been over forty feet high, we caught
sight of our lost property. Those trunks which
happened to be at the bottom were crushed as
flat as newspapers. I had the list of the contents
written in German, and as soon as the officials
were satisfied that we had claims, they handed
it over for nine marks. This was the one we
had lost on the 2nd of August. It speaks
well for their organisation that we should have
recovered it intact as late as the 14th of October,
and so far from the place where we had lost it.
By the time we reached the hotel, we found
that Cook's had recovered the other. This we
took as a good augury, and we revelled in our
good luck. All this time there was the haunting dread that we should not be able to proceed
any farther on our travels. As soon as Conrad
could put his foot to the ground, he paid a visit
to the American Ambassador (the late Mr.
Penfield), who proved himself a true friend in
need. He managed to get us permission to
proceed to the Italian frontier. It was only a
verbal permission, and no one could give us
more. Never shall I forget standing in the
rain when we reached the frontier and watching
Conrad's face. He was positively ashen ; then

he suddenly launched out into German—a language he had not spoken since he was a tiny boy. The official, who obviously was quite ignorant of what he was looking at, fingered our papers, adopting a knowing air, and, blessed relief, allowed us to go. He gruffly warned us that the Italians might make trouble as we had come from the district where there had been some cholera.

After this we reached Milan with comparatively little trouble, and our minds were set more at ease by the knowledge that England was still holding her own and not doing it too badly. We stayed a week in Milan, and from there we journeyed to Genoa. Here we were fortunate enough to get a passage in a Dutch steamer, and we reached England on the 3rd of November. A chill feeling of dismay came over me at Fenchurch Street Station on seeing the taxis with their grim behests to all to join up. We had crossed the Italian frontier only one short week before orders were received from Germany to hold us back till the end of the war. We had had a narrow escape.

VI

WAR

HOW to describe the changed aspect of that part of England—the nearest, as a matter of fact, to the French fighting-line! One responded to the familiar features of the land and one was awed by the sight of temporary camps that had sprung up here and there, dotting the friendly rural landscape which one knew so well, and by the sight of the columns of Kitchener's infantry moving along the roads, on their route marches. Our house being situated within the limits of the Dover command, we could hear all day long, and sometimes at night, the sound of heavy guns at Dover, in Sheerness, and in the estuary of the Thames. Of course one knew it was practice firing, but all the same it put a stress into one's life—brought, as it were, physically the fact of the war home to one. The faint tremor of the earth and the slight trembling of the window-panes became part of one's daily life.   One did not ever get quite used to them.

Our eldest boy had to curb his impatience, in deference to his·father's will, and on the assurance, which he implicitly trusted, that he would not be too late to play his part in whatever fate reserved for his country.   Ultimately, in August 1915, he got his commission of 2nd Lieutenant and his instructions to join the depôt at Grove Park.   In that envelope from the War Office there were various other papers and also a new cheque-book—the first cheque-book of his life—the symbol, as it were, of his independent existence.   The first time I saw him in khaki I caught my breath, and I realised for the first time what the war-anguish meant ; but I dare say I concealed it creditably, being helped in that effort by the loud lamentations of all the maids, for whom the sight was altogether too much.   All of them had known him as a schoolboy, and one of them, indeed, ever since he was two years of age.

On the day he left home to join the depôt in Grove Park he was seventeen and a half years old and looked very youthful.   Conrad, whose mission it generally was to take him to his various schools and leave him behind there, went with him on that occasion too.   He did not go all the way to the camp, however.   He got out of the car at Bromley, at the railway station, and came home by train. He told me that the look of ecstatic happiness on the boy's face was enough to frighten anybody.

Before the end of the year we heard that he had been appointed to one of the new howitzer batteries, and he left England for the front two or three days before his eighteenth birthday. The Christmas before he left we went to Portsmouth, where he was then stationed, and spent a few days there, and that was the last sight we had of him for more than a year.

Not for worlds would I have had it otherwise, yet I have heard women lament that they have no son "to give to the war" (it was quite a stock phrase), and I wished sometimes that they could have known, if only for one moment, the anguish of parents who were able "to give a son to the war." Conrad and I used to look at each other every time the post brought us a hurriedly scrawled letter or a field post card. Any one might have been the last. Everywhere around us sons, husbands, brothers, were reported killed, wounded, or missing. It came to this at last, that one had almost a feeling of shame that one's son escaped when so many of other poor people's sons were dying every day.

Conrad and I had at least the comfort of having John with us, and I had need of every comfort I could get, because just at that time I was not feeling at all well. And presently my husband, on the invitation of the Admiralty, went away to visit some of our naval bases. I must say that I felt his absence very much, though of course I did not say a single discouraging word. And here I must record one of my personal successes—obtained only at a distance, it is true—a success of mingled hilarity and esteem which pleased Conrad very much.

He wrote to me one day from Lowestoft to tell me that he was going out very soon for an experience of mine-sweeping, and, of course, as usual, I answered by return of post. Conrad received my letter early in the morning, and at breakfast, in the officers' mess-room at the base, he pulled it out of his pocket and said, " I wrote to my wife telling her I was about to go out mine-sweeping for a time, and this is what she says." And he read aloud amidst a general silence, " ' Do be careful and don't catch cold.' " Thereupon there was an enormous burst of laughter all round the table, and words of commendation for what they proclaimed " the right kind of wife." But what else could I have said?—unless I had made a fuss, which

would have been stupid and odious! And
my recommendation was useful, too, because
Conrad, like a good, obedient husband, went
up to High Street at once and bought himself
a thick jersey, of which he told me he was
very glad all the time he was out with the
sweepers.

Our eldest boy's first leave was in 1917,
and he was at home on his nineteenth birthday. I looked at him with a certain wonder.
He had developed physically, and looked
strangely mature in every way. Only his
manner with me remained what it had been
in his schooldays. I had fifteen days of fearful joy. . . .

The days of parting after leave do not bear
much talking about. I must do ourselves the
justice of saying that we kept smiling all the
time, but each of the days ahead seemed in
prospect more than one could bear. It was
during this time that Conrad finished his story,
" The Shadow-Line," which he dedicated " To
Borys and all his generation." This dedication
used to trouble me all the time my boy was
at the front. There seemed something ominous
in it, though of course the line alluded to
has no relation to the passage from life to
death, but symbolises the passage from the
irresponsible early youth to the wider self-

realisation and the responsibilities of man-
hood.

In the course of 1918, on the advice of our
doctor, growing uneasy at the state of my knee,
we consulted the eminent surgeon, Sir Robert
Jones, now one of the family's most loved and
respected friends, who operated on me in July.
We had, naturally, to go to London for that,
and there I had to the full the opportunity of
tasting the emotions of lying helpless in bed
on the top floor of a nursing-home while some
of the heaviest air-raids on London took
place. All that, however, was as nothing in
comparison with the pleasure of seeing our
eldest boy, to whom a special leave was
granted for the purpose of being near me at
that trying time.

Our boy hastened back to the front, to be
transferred with his battery to General
Plummer's army and participate in the battles
in Flanders and in the general advance.

Meantime we had returned to Capel, and
Conrad, notwithstanding his anxiety about myself and the state of affairs at the front, went
on steadily with his novel, " The Arrow of
Gold," which is the second of his war-time
books.

Early in October a War Office telegram was
delivered at our house, expressing the regret

of the Secretary of State that our boy had been
severely shell-shocked and gassed during the
Second Army's advance on the Menin road.
Next day a letter from himself arrived, dated
from a Rouen hospital. It was very reassuring,
and ended with the words, " In a week I shall
be back with my battery again." But this
was the end of the war for him.

Afterwards we learned the details, which
accounted fully for his state as described by
the War Office. On that day, which was his
last day of active service, he was first buried
under the ruins of a farmhouse which had
received a direct hit from a German shell, and
in which everybody but himself was killed.
Some of the men of his ammunition column and
some of the gunners dug him out, with all his
limbs whole, and apparently not feeling any
effect from the gases he had breathed. He told
us that he never lost consciousness all that
time.

Two or three hours afterwards, the retreating
Germans having got the accurate range of the
road on which his column was arrested, he
ordered his men into a deep ditch, to take
shelter on one side of it. After seeing his men
in there, he and his sergeant took shelter too,
when almost immediately a German H.E. shell
landed on the rear slope and completely buried

7

in mud more than half the men. That was the last thing he remembered clearly before finding himself in a Canadian first-line hospital, where the nurses were extremely good to him.

The consequences of the shock developed slowly, and all we heard of him was the news that he was being moved from one hospital to another. Our anxieties were kept alive all the time, and meantime I had managed to get bronchitis, which laid me up, and added much to the strain from which Conrad was suffering. But he had managed to finish the " Arrow of Gold," and also to devote himself to the task of nursing me with an unremitting care.

One day in early December, at dusk, we heard a car come to the front door, and Conrad, who had been reading to me, got up and went to see who it could be. Then, as I lay there wondering and listening, with that sort of permanent anxiety which belonged to one's natural state in these days, I heard my husband's exclamation of surprise, and directly afterwards a deep voice asking anxiously, " Where's Mum ? "

With his arrival home, returned to us whole certainly, but very far from well, as we soon discovered, I closed my eyes in deep thankfulness, and tasted the first moment of real peace for years. The cold hand of dread lying for so many days on our, I hope, undismayed hearts was removed by the sound of his voice asking for me.   And on that moment of crowning mercy I will bring to an end my recollections of our later years.

VII

MY RELATION TO THE BOOKS

MY husband's books were to me as so many children, so to speak, and each in turn should have its place in these recollections. There is attached to one and all some tender remembrance and unforgotten episode. It was Conrad's unfailing custom to make me a present when each book was finished, and those presents varied in money-value according to the state of our finances. Sometimes a promise was all that was possible— a promise to be redeemed later by some stroke of fortune or lucky find in some unexpected place.

"Almayer's Folly" was written before I knew him—written in many strange places, under changing conditions. It survived only by the merest chance its many adventures, and got itself finished, or at least nearly finished, in the home of an early friend, Mr. E. L. Sanderson — on his father's sermon paper.

Some chapters were written in shabby, sordid lodgings on the bank of the river Thames, in the little village of Greenhythe. Conrad once showed the house to me when we were paying a visit to Borys, then a *Worcester* cadet. Although that little place so close to the river was sordid in the extreme, there was a charm, even to me, in the view of the swiftly running water, in the group of dirty urchins clustered round the boats—poorly clad little mortals, who were as much at home in a boat as any old salt, and who could handle an oar as well.

This first book is the only one that bears on its fly-leaf my full maiden name, and I can recall my pride when it was presented to me quite early in our acquaintance. A mutual friend introduced us early in November 1894. I think my first feeling was one of surprise and awe. To me ours was certainly a strange friendship. Not only because Conrad was the first foreigner I had ever known intimately, but he was also the first grown man I had met who appeared to take a particular interest in me.

Several months elapsed between our fourth and fifth meeting—months in which I heard little of the strange and courteous gentleman, the author of my inscribed copy of "Almayer's Folly." In fact, the book was the one concrete fact left me to prove that our acquaintance had been no dream.

Our next meeting was not long before the next book, " The Outcast of the Islands," was finished ; but our friendship had by this time become much more intimate. We had reached the stage when he became a frequent visitor to my home. Even in those days I seemed to have influence over him—an interest for him perhaps I should rather have said—and my curiosity about this second venture appeared to please him . . . when I grew bold enough to show it. It was not long after this that he appeared one evening with a bulky package of manuscript from which he suggested I should read him some pages right away. That night was my first experience of his characteristic impatience ; and after all these years, I can still feel as I felt that night, trembling with pleased interest, and with my mouth as dry as a cinder. He sat a few feet from me, his compelling eyes fastened on my face. I was even then conscious of something restless in him, of a sort of inward fire that robbed me of nearly all my powers of speech. I read on, stumbling over the corrections that interlined the closely typed pages. Sometimes he interrupted me, urging me to disregard this or that pencilled sentence : " That is not going to stand—never mind it—start three lines lower—over leaf, over leaf." After a time he gave a short, impatient laugh and said irritably, drawing the pages none too gently from my hands : " Speak distinctly ; if you're tired, say so ; don't eat your words. You English are all alike, you make the same sound for every letter."

These words and his gesture of exasperation almost reduced me to tears. He sat with his face buried in his hands for some few moments, and with a mighty effort I recovered myself somewhat. After that I frequently read his manuscript aloud to him, taking great pains to speak the words as he seemed to wish, and passing as sensible comments as I was capable of making. It must be remembered that I was strange to literature, and too anxious perhaps to appear at my ease. Then came the day when the book was finished and I received my first present to mark the event. A little ruby and pearl bracelet—a great treasure—now, alas ! too small for me to wear.

This book was to have appeared in November 1895, but the stereo plates were burnt in a big printer's fire, and the publication was delayed till the year we were married. In fact, the book was born only a day or so before our wedding on 24th March 1896.

It was in the early December 1895 that by medical advice he went to stay for a month in La Rosera, Champell, to take a cure. During these weeks of absence, his letters were frequent, and I saw that our friendship would soon undergo a change. When he returned, we picked up the threads of our life with perhaps a little restraint. Then came that never-to-be-forgotten day when we became engaged. Surely such a compact has been seldom entered upon in quite the same manner. We had spent a long morning in the National Picture Gallery ; we had engaged ourselves, and afterwards we had had some lunch in a strange restaurant. Was it one of these events, or was it the combination of all three that produced such disastrous results ? The question remained a matter of argument between us afterwards. Instead of following our plan of taking a long drive into the country, we each returned to our separate homes in haste. Awful sensations had come over us both at the same moment. I caught sight of my own face passing a shop window, and a horrified glance at Conrad discovered on his the same expression of acute suffering. It needed little urging to persuade me to let him drive me home. We parted hurriedly at my door, and he hastily re-entered the hansom, which drove rapidly away, urged to even greater speed by a hand waved frantically through the trap in the roof.

I said no word at home. After a third day had passed without a word from him, I felt very humiliated. I was tortured by the thought that perhaps he had already repented of his offer. It was surely a strange proposal of marriage. He had begun by announcing that he had not very long to live and no intention of having children ; but such as his life was (his shrug was very characteristic), he thought we might spend a few happy years together. At the end of the third day an invitation came for my mother and for me to lunch with him near Victoria Station. The interview he had with her must have been conducted on much the same lines, judging by her artless remark to me a little later, " that she didn't quite see why he wished to get married." But a climax was reached a day or so later when he demanded that we should be married in less than six weeks and go abroad.

Those weeks passed very quickly. My time was fully occupied with my preparations, and I was not a little sad, for I was to be the first of my family to leave home. My mother made no secret of her distress and dismay at the prospect of my leaving her. A few days before our wedding-day, he came and solemnly insisted that all my precious letters, those few letters he had written when he was staying in Geneva, should be burnt, and what was more, he himself superintended the sacrifice. Not one escaped. When it came to leaving my home after we were married, Conrad was greatly disconcerted because my numerous brothers and sisters gave vent to their feelings in howls. " Good heavens ! " he said to my mother, " I would never have got married if I had known this would happen."

The first book he began after we were married was " The Rescue," and this, as I have told, was begun just three weeks after we were married, in our little peasant house on Ile Grande, where we spent our honeymoon.

The next book to be published was the " Nigger of the *Narcissus.*" This one was also begun during our sojourn on the island. The opening words of this book were written while he was beginning to recover from his first attack of gout after marriage, which I have already described. One day, I suppose I had been dozing in my chair, I heard his voice sounding in a far-away and curious tone. " Wait ! " he was saying. There was a pause, and again he murmured, " Wait . . . James, Wait ! " I naturally asked him if he wanted any one. His answer showed that his mind

was full of the book he had been writing:
" James Wait is the name of the sick nigger,"
he said—" a big buck nigger. You'll hear
enough about him by and by." A wonderful
lot of tenderness and sympathy has gone to
the making of that book. Old Singleton, and
even Donkin, have a little share of my affection.
I have often delighted Conrad by quoting the
passage, " I think I'll go and sleep in the fore-
top-stay-sail ter-night " ; I could picture the
queer little impudent cockney Donkin trailing
the corner of his dirty blanket behind him
across the deck.

Glancing at my copy in which we pasted
some early cuttings, I came upon a review from
the *Army and Navy Gazette*, 19th of February
1897. I found that Conrad had underlined
these words : " In the main the story deals with
the curious effect produced upon the crew of
the *Narcissus* by the nigger, who is the hero of
the story, *and this in itself is a psychological
study of great value and interest* ; but the writer
also shows a keen eye for scenery, *a knowledge
of seamanship which is rather surprising in
modern fiction*, and a certain broad acquaintance
with the feelings of the seaman hardly equalled
by the veteran Mr. Clark Russell himself."

" Tales of Unrest " followed next in order of
publication, although some of the stories were

written some time before. " The Idiots " were familiar objects to me, as I have already said, for nearly six months. We knew all of them quite well. We used to meet them on the Brittany roads when we drove to the mainland, and on our walks ; and I have seen them all too often in my dreams. Clad in shapeless long black garments, their arms folded, with their hands inserted in their loose sleeves, and their faces set in a vacant stare, they used to shuffle up and down the road near their farmhouse home. As the cattle would return to shelter when the evening came on, so these pathetic figures would drift homewards when night fell. Sometimes we would come upon them sprawling in the deep ditch, their bodies hidden in the long grass. I have seen them tossing a piece of crust of bread in the air and catching it in their mouths like dogs. In all there were seven of these creatures—two girls and five boys. I once pointed out to Conrad that there were two more than he had said in his story. His curt answer that five were enough in all conscience silenced me effectually. I believe he really enjoyed writing " The Lagoon " ; to me the treatment resembles the " Rescue," a similarity that is not only due to the fact that the setting is the same. I seem to detect in both books the same mood.

The " Outpost of Progress " was written in a somewhat savage mood. It was the one story he refused to allow me to begin to copy till he had written the last word. He then handed me the manuscript with a request that I should do it as quickly as possible, " I want it out of the house ! "

The next in order of the stories in " Tales of Unrest " was that beautiful story " Karain." I remember he was a very long time writing this ; several attempts were made, only to be suddenly torn and flung in the wastepaper-basket. Then for days the few pages that had survived would lie on the table, the corners of the paper turned up, ragged, and twisted. One morning, as I stood beside him, I saw him making some queer designs in the margin of a fresh page, on which were written a few lines. I stood silent but deeply interested, held there by a gentle request, " Don't go away ; wait a moment." I waited, and slowly out of the maze of lines a face appeared, grew, and developed. " ' Karain ' ; do you like the look of him, Jess ? "

This manuscript was a great treasure, and I was very reluctant to part from it. I can never be certain whether or not that little sketch of the head of " Karain " went with that manuscript on its ill-fated journey to New York or not. Somehow I think it must have done, for all my searching through the mountain of papers has never succeeded in bringing it to light. It may be, of course, that he destroyed it long before he finished the story.

Then came the long novel, " Lord Jim." Although this is the longest book I copied, I became almost word perfect in the greater part of it. I could quote whole passages from memory. Conrad himself has said that he has deliberately crammed as much character and episode into it as it would hold. He thought himself that the actual tale itself did not justify its length. He had at first only intended to write a short story concerned only with the pilgrim-ship—nothing more ; but the book as it stands never seemed to me too long.

It was the days, weeks, even months, when he could not write a line, that held for us the greatest worry and stress. Many times I have tried to coax him to put the work out of his mind completely and come with me for some little jaunt, urging that rest must be good for his mind. Conrad could never be persuaded. He would always declare that he must sit tight to wait for an inspiration. After the first two or three years, when our fortunes allowed us to invest in a pony and trap, I did sometimes carry my point and coax him into taking a drive with me. It was he who taught me to drive, in fact. But I won't go so far as to say that I enjoyed the lessons altogether; Conrad was an impatient and exacting teacher. Still, I had many hours of real enjoyment when I became efficient.

There were days when I perceived that Conrad was not in the mood for driving himself, but unfortunately those were the times when he would obstinately refuse to let me have the reins. His mind miles away, he would suddenly clutch the reins and administer a sharp cut with the whip. This happened once when the old mare we had was carefully picking her way down a rather steep hill. It was a high two-wheeled cart, and the sudden jerk of the reins and the stroke of the whip took the animal by surprise. She started forward and crossed her feet. Down she went like a stone, and Conrad sailed out of the trap like a huge frog. He was wearing a dark brown havelock and he landed on the mare's head, whip and reins in hand; even his glasses remained on his nose, and his hat was still on his head. Almost as if I had been waiting for him to land first, I followed; but my landing was less fortunate. I fell half in and half out of the cart, with my bad knee against the dashboard. My position amongst the horse's heels alarmed Conrad, and he began feverishly trying to drag me clear. My

chief anxiety was the child strapped at the
back, who, with the groom, was surveying the
scene from above.   I feared that the mare in trying to get up might rise under the shaft and
turn the cart over.   To my great relief, however, she rose quietly and stood still, cropping
the grass at the side of the road.   The extent
of Conrad's injuries, I was thankful to discover,
was only a little of the skin barked off his glove.
I was badly bruised, and the nervous shock had
made me appear to have two very black eyes.

In later years, when he drove a car, my state
of mind was very apprehensive.   One day he
took a sharp corner in an ancient single-cylinder
Cadillac, very high on its wheels, at the rate
of 20 miles an hour, and brought up against a
gate with terrific force.   The little John, seated
beside him, greatly awed, was told on no account
to tell me of the incident, but on their return
home the chauffeur's white face caught my
instant attention.   His answer, when I asked
him what was wrong, amused me very much:
" Madame, I've been nearer heaven this morning than I ever want to be again."

To a man like Conrad a car was rather " a
stiff proposition," as our American friends say,
and my feelings at the end of a drive were invariably those of thankfulness that at least
another drive was successfully over.   On one

occasion he returned with a friend he had met
at the station, with the right mudguard hanging down like the broken wing of a bird. His
only remark in answer to my concerned inquiry
was, " Oh ! but, Jess, I know the cow I hit will
be tender for weeks."

The book that followed " Lord Jim " was a
collaboration with Ford Madox Hueffer, who
on this occasion arrived with his wife and child,
and stayed a fortnight or more. The old farmhouse was not adapted for the shelter of two
families, or capable of providing seclusion for
the two authors engaged upon even such a book
as " The Inheritors." No doubt our guests
suffered quite as much as I did. I had often
to hold myself in strict restraint, but I had a
motive in my self-sacrifice. I knew that in
those days Conrad found F. M. H. a mental
stimulus, but he was not the literary godfather
he claims to have been at any time. It was
fortunate that the two children, their girl and
our boy, were very good friends ; Christina
was at that time nearly three, and Borys about
two.

The next volume is perhaps more mine than
any other ; it is the one that is dedicated to
me—" Youth." The book takes its title from
the first story in the book. As Conrad says in
his author's note : " Even before appearing

8

in book form, ' Youth ' was very well received.
It lies on me to confess at last, and this is as
good a place for it as any other, that I have
been all my life—all my two lives—the spoiled
adopted child of Great Britain and even of the
Empire ; for it was Australia that gave me my
first command. I break out into this declara-
tion not because of a lurking tendency to
megalomania, but, on the contrary, as a man
who has no very notable illusions about himself.
I follow the instincts of vain-glory and humility
natural to mankind. For it can hardly be
denied that it is not their own deserts that men
are most proud of, but rather of their prodigious
luck, of their marvellous fortune ; of that in
their lives for which thanks and sacrifices must
be offered on the altars of the inscrutable gods."

This story of old Captain Beard, and his
tragic first command, is very pathetic to me.
I used to picture his despair, his terrible disappointment, when the ship had to put back,
first for repairs, and again because the crew
refused to sail on a ship the rats had left—the
old superstition that in this case was so amply
justified in the end.

The second story in this volume is, of course,
practically autobiographical, and the little
diary, recently published in " Last Essays," was
Conrad's constant companion, his silent com-

panion, during those terrible months in darkest Africa. Here it was that he met first the notorious Sir Roger Casement. He has told me many times of his first sight of him, walking down the hill with his dog Pat in his arms. The poor animal had worn all the skin off his pads during some long march following his master.

The last story in this book is the "End of the Tether." The greater part of it was written against time in a little cottage in Winchelsea, near the house of the Hueffers. Conrad would remain writing far into the night, burning the midnight oil, and refreshed at intervals by Ford Madox Hueffer, who would appear from time to time armed with a bottle and a few sandwiches, or biscuits and cheese. Almost at daybreak he would retire, worn out, and I would take up the work with the typewriter. A little after eight the groom would appear mounted on our trusty old mare, ready to ride to the post with the typescript.

It was a weird existence ours, during those weeks, and the people of the cottage afforded me not a little fun—when I had time to enjoy it. The household was a strange one: a lady whom we had at first taken to be a widow, but who was in reality the wife of a man she had divorced in Africa. This gentleman was now installed as handy-man and cook in the house. There must have been some secrecy about his presence there, probably owing to the fact that the wife was receiving some outside help from her mother. I conclude this to have been the case by a remark I overheard one day. One of the younger children asked his mother, " Mummy, granny is coming to-day; is daddy father or cook ? "

Then, in order of publication, followed " Romance," the second product of collaboration. Once again the two authors worked in the room beneath my bedroom. I must confess that I could never read " The Inheritors," and what I did read of it, I have failed utterly to understand.

For many of its pages Conrad is wholly responsible, and the interest is intense and varied all through. " Romance " was written in the two homes, turn and turn about ; but in Winchelsea we always had rooms in a cottage close at hand, while at Pent, being far from any other house, we had to put up Heuffer and often his family. I have often lain awake, listening to the voices from the room below raised either in argument or enthusiastic assent. Frequently F. M. H., who was very tall, would pause while pacing the room and bang his fist on the oaken beam that crossed the ceiling.

One night Borys, who was sleeping in his little bed in my room, awoke with a start, and said to me fearfully, " Mama dear, moo-cows down there."

The year 1902 saw the birth of " Typhoon." I have before me the little edition published by the Knickerbocker Press (Putnams, London and New York) and illustrated by Maurice Greiffenhagen. This edition, I believe, is rather rare. I remember Conrad was extremely pleased with these illustrations, and in this matter my husband was extremely difficult to please.

Speaking in " A Personal Record " of " Typhoon," and in explanation of what his aim had been in writing it, Conrad says : " An historian of hearts is not an historian of emotions, yet he penetrates further, restrained as he may be, since his aim is to reach the very font of laughter and tears. The sight of human affairs deserves admiration and pity. They are worthy of respect too. And he is not insensible who pays them the undemonstrative tribute of a sigh which is not a sob, and of a smile which is not a grin."

This book, " Typhoon," contains also the story, " Amy Foster." F. M. H. claims that the plot was his in " A Personal Remembrance." The only foundation for this claim is that there is in Winchelsea churchyard a grave which bears on the head-stone no name, but recording the fact that the bodies of one or two foreign seamen are buried there, after being washed ashore. I very well remember F. M. H. pointing this grave out to us one day. This fact and a story—a mere fragment heard during a meal in a country inn—gave Conrad the material he needed. The actual character, Amy Foster, was for many years in our service, and it was her animal-like capacity for sheer uncomplaining endurance that inspired Conrad. That and nothing else.

The story, " Falk," was culled from a short paragraph in a newspaper which had some relation to an episode known to Conrad many years before, while he was at sea. I remember I was quite physically sick when I typed those pages. Sick with disgust at the idea of human beings having been cooked. I thought of this story many years after when, during the war, Conrad, in a fit of economy, decided to use a flint and steel cigarette lighter. In a fit of abstraction he had replaced the thing in his pocket without extinguishing it. Soon his secretary, who was sitting by his side at work, remarked with a disgusted sniff, " Oh, Mr. Conrad, there's a very nasty smell of cooking in here ! "

The last story in that volume we neither of us liked very much. It belongs, with two others written much later, to those stories Conrad could never find a good word for. Those two others were the "Black Mate," of which I suggested the gist, and, later, "The Inn of the Two Witches." I used to try to coax him to regard these three stories with a rather more indulgent eye, urging the good points which they each undoubtedly possess. But no; at the second and third reading, Conrad condemned them with such finality that I forbore henceforth to defend them.

VIII

"NOSTROMO" AND OTHER STORIES

"NOSTROMO" next made its appearance in book form in 1904, and its reception was perhaps the greatest disappointment — literary disappointment — Conrad ever had. He used to say it was "a dead frost." It was, too, the first book he attempted to dramatise. A young Polish friend and Conrad had prepared—prepared is the only word possible—quite a lot of the book in the form of a play. I never knew exactly why the project was never completed. Of all his books it is the one which was least based upon facts. It is a great work to have constructed upon so slight an actual foundation.

The next book, "The Mirror of the Sea," was begun under totally different conditions. The greater part was written away from home. One or two of the "papers" were dictated by Conrad to Hueffer, because by this time I had become much more helpless and the first active

measures were being taken to cure my knee.
Conrad has told me how, during the three hours
which my first operation lasted, finding it
impossible to remain in the sitting-room of the
nursing-home, he rushed outside and walked up
and down, that dull November morning. He
paced to and fro without being aware of his
surroundings, and finally, as he himself said,
" brought up close against the nose of an old
dray horse." He stood patting the animal,
and presently the drayman, stowing the remains
of his meal in a capacious pocket, accosted him
with the remark that his " hoss being broken-
winded was very expensive to feed—can't give
'im any 'ay." Conrad came to himself with
a start, and handed the man half a crown for
an extra feed.

Much of this book he brought to me to read,
and we both had a very tender spot in our
hearts for those pages. One reviewer made
use of rather an apt heading : " When Conrad
holds his Mirror to the sea." I think the
" Tremolino " is almost my favourite. It refers
to the most adventurous part of Conrad's life,
to the days when he was a mere youth and was
engaged in smuggling on the coast of Spain.
He has told me how, after he had steered his
vessel on to the rocks, ripping the bottom out
of her, he and the other smugglers had hidden

for days in a low posada, in an underground
cellar that was more like a cavern, till the
authorities had given up the search. It was
after this that he, with some half-dozen others,
found themselves one evening in Marseilles,
with but ten or twenty francs between them.
They had all dined well, and when the time
came to pay, all turned out their pockets.
The eldest carefully collected the coins and,
turning to Conrad, then a youth of under
nineteen, bade him go and gamble with the
little store. For over an hour those other
fellows, all older than the boy they had sent to
take his chance, sat round the table jesting and
waiting. After a time he returned and, closing
the door gently, advanced towards the table.
The leader rose to his feet licking his dry lips.
Without the least elation the boy poured his
winnings out on the table. This was his first
experience at a gaming table, and his gains were
more than enough to pay for the dinner, give
a liberal tip to the waiter, and leave quite a
comfortable little sum for the pockets of each
of the adventurers. Conrad said he found
some one pushing his own share into his hand,
and still bewildered, he made his way out into
the street in company with the rest.

He had one other adventure in Marseilles
about the same time—I imagine with the same

jovial spirits as companions. This was after a dinner—and a drink. Conrad had hired a two-horse closed carriage to meet them after the dinner. Some spirit moved those young men to force the coachman to climb on the slippery roof, where he lay sprawling helplessly, his whole energy devoted to keeping his balance. The driver being disposed of, Conrad and one of the others mounted the box, one had the reins but the other had the whip. The drive was a wild one; the horses, urged by the whip and wild shouts, tore down the street at breakneck speed. Conrad gave no very clear account of the end of this adventure, but he told me it involved some considerable energy on the part of several gendarmes and a not inconsiderable fine all round.

Several times while he was writing his early books, Conrad made several half - hearted attempts to escape from the world of letters and return once again to his old mistress, the sea. When we first married he was trying to negotiate the purchase of a sailing-ship, the wooden barque *Windermere*, a vessel which was finally lost off Dover some twelve years later. I remember going to Grangemouth with him, my young sister, and a friend, to look at her. This friend, himself a master mariner, shook his head ominously when he saw from the quay one or two gulls sitting on the mast-heads. We went all over the vessel ; her big saloon had suffered severely from the fierce handling, it seemed, of a lot of madmen. The wilfulness of the damage was unmistakable ; all the cushions were torn and the woodwork broken. It appears that the vessel had been left to several of the relatives of the owner, whose disagreement had been violent. Then again, some two years later, when Borys was two weeks old, Conrad once again felt the call of the sea. This time he went alone to look at a small vessel ; he had golden visions of trading with her in the East after the manner, I believe, of his beloved character, Tom Lingard. How such a life would have suited us with a young child I scarcely dared to think. It was understood that I was to accompany him with the baby. Only once more did he entertain the hope of returning to his old life. Borys was then nearly old enough to go to school. Apart from the fact that by this time I had grown sufficiently bold to demur and point out that he was now well established as an author and coming into his own, there was also the great difficulty I now had in getting about. Finally, he gave up the idea for ever, and settled down to his writing for good, though the delightful project of making a company of seafaring friends and taking a long voyage in a sailing yacht some day, still dangled before us. As it happened, the only time he spent again at sea was during the war, on that trip of a fortnight or so, aboard the mystery ship, with Commander Sutherland.

" The Secret Agent " was written, as I have already mentioned, under circumstances that might well have appalled the stoutest heart. It had more difficulties in the way of its birth than any of the others. It was written partly while I had to undergo a serious operation— this in itself was more than enough to give its author little zest for creative work ; and it was finally finished, curiously enough, in the very hotel in Geneva where Conrad had stayed when he had gone to Switzerland to take a cure in his bachelor days more than once. I cannot recall that time, the weeks we spent there, without a shudder, for, as I have said, it was by the merest chance that either of the boys lived to return to England.

I don't think Conrad ever quite forgave me for trying to persuade him not to dramatise that book. I urged him earnestly not to attempt to make a play out of any book he had already written. It seemed to me that a work conceived as a play would have a much better chance of success. It was only when I saw how his heart was set upon the idea that

I said no more. When it was produced with such poor success, he said to me, " You need not think I have given up the idea of having a play to my credit; wait and see ! "

" A Set of Six," the next book, contains some very remarkable short stories; of their origin I knew less than of any others, perhaps. " Gaspar Ruiz " is surely—for the cinema—one of the best stories Conrad ever wrote. To each of these tales he has given a sub-title. " The Informer " he called an ironic tale; this was written under very great difficulties and many distractions. This one, and the one entitled " An Anarchist," cost their author great mental suffering.

Borys caught scarlet fever a week or ten days before our trip to town. This trip was to be my reward for weeks of hard work and much anxiety, for Conrad had had one attack of gout after another. (It was a matter of argument always between us, which was the cause and which the effect—did gout produce irritability, or *vice versa* ? This was never decided.) I can see Conrad now, carrying the boy wrapped in a blanket down to the waiting ambulance; over anxious, he accidentally knocked the child's head against the lintel of the door. His distress at this little mishap was, as usual, out of all proportion. The boy blinked back his tears and declared, "It didn't hurt—not much, Dada dear." Then followed those six or seven weeks in a very smelly, uncomfortable lodging, the only refuge we were able to get anywhere near the nursing-home. I was to nurse the boy in the day, and we had a very nice nurse for the night. I have thought since that nowadays I should not have been allowed to do so. The doctor in attendance never even asked me if I had had the disease. I can only remember one little incident that could be called by any stretch of imagination humorous in that time. Conrad developed an acute attack of gout, and my nights were passed sitting on two chairs, because my gouty patient could not endure any one to come near the bed.

In the intervals between painful attacks of gout these two stories were getting themselves written : "The Duel," under less strenuous circumstances, and also "The Brute." The original of "Il Conde" was a Polish gentleman whom we met in Capri. His friendliness and courtesy made our stay much more enjoyable than it would otherwise have been, and we needed some compensation, for the journey had been a big undertaking, both for my husband and myself. I shall never forget the morning we started from the flat in Addison Road. Our journey was arranged to fit in

beautifully, and carrying-chairs for me were
ordered along the line of our route. I was
taken abroad like a bale of goods, taken to
Capri to learn to walk again for the second time
in my life. Poor Conrad ! Looking back on
that journey, I see how very little fitted he was
to have had such a responsibility even in those
days. From the start we were unfortunate. I
was perfectly helpless, and the first thing that
went awry was the loss of a favourite pair of
glasses ; neither of the other pairs I produced
would he consider, even when I pointed out
that the missing ones were terribly rusty. We
were late for the train ; my chair was a wheeled
one (no good). There was great difficulty in
getting me on board at Dover. The bearers
nearly deposited me in the water between the
vessel and the quay. A horrified howl of dismay
went up from the passengers when they saw
my perilous position perched up on the rail of
the slanting gangway. The trouble was due
to one of the men getting his hand pinched
between the chair and the rail. I admired his
fortitude, for the pain must indeed have been
pretty severe (I am, alas ! no fairy) ; his
language was not very choice, and he did not
offer his apology before he pocketed a sub-
stantial tip. It might have been a very un-
dignified tragedy. The rest of the long journey

was tolerable till we got to Rome. Here my nurse and a few noisy but inefficient Italians, not understanding their instructions, removed the chair, and left me hanging by my arms to the train. It was quite a little time before I managed to make myself understood. Conrad suffered much more than I did, each time. His imagination was at work, while my only thought was how long I could hang on before I dropped back on the platform. Our arrival in Naples was at least a pause in our adventures. Here we were delayed for a week on account of the rough weather. Then, one bright, sunny day, I made my uncomfortable passage in an ordinary wooden chair, with my foot slung to my neck in a black satin sling. I don't remember what time we left Naples, but it was a gorgeous moonlight night when we reached Capri. We made the next stage of our journey in the little carriages as far as horsed traffic could go ; then in another chair, and closely clasping two very garlicky Italians, I was transported up innumerable stone steps to the little villa belonging to the priest's father. My first thought was how on earth should I ever get down those steps again ! Here we lived four months, and more manuscript was written. Poor Conrad had a bad time with his teeth, which had now begun to worry him in earnest. He would try no

9

remedy suggested, but kept his mouth full of
cold water when the pain was bad.   One night
he lay with his poor head on my shoulder and
his mouth full of water (I keeping awake and
holding the glass ready to pass to him as he
wanted it). He would fill his mouth, hand me the
glass, and fall asleep, and the water would run
all over me. I was soaked before the morning.
When he finally roused himself sufficiently to
be aware that he was uncomfortable, he declared
we had been sleeping in a damp bed.

Our return trip, by way of a tramp steamer
from Naples to Marseilles, was a laughable
contrast to our journey to Italy just four
months ago. My nurse had by this time returned to England, and we three—Conrad, the
boy, and I—were alone. We enjoyed the three
last weeks of our stay, and when he suggested
returning in a tramp steamer, I was perfectly
willing. I had by this time discarded my
crutches, which were sent, together with sundry
earthen pots and pans, curtains, etc., by
baggage train, and only reached us some two
months after we arrived home. I was rather
appalled when I saw the height of the vessel's
side which I had to climb, by means of a rope-
ladder, from the little boat tossing at its foot.
However, the captain grabbed me tightly, and
assisted me on board, and we had quite a jolly

three or four days as the sole passengers,
except for the fact that Conrad discovered
that he had mislaid his wallet containing
practically all the money we had left. As we
called nowhere till we arrived in Marseilles,
our chance of reclaiming it from the café in
Naples (where Conrad was confident that he
must have left it) was small indeed. It was
not until we had been two days aboard that
he confessed what was troubling him. My
natural question, " Are you sure it isn't in one
of your pockets ? " called forth a veritable
explosion. " Of course ! I knew you would
say that. As if I were such a blamed fool not
to have looked everywhere ! It's gone, and
all your lamentations won't make any difference.
We shall have to hang out till I can get hold
of Pinker. Damn nuisance, to say the least
of it ! Damn ! "

That night I waited till he was sound asleep,
and then quietly removed all the clothing I could
lay my hands on to the cabin I shared with
the child. I dared not let him see me searching,
after his emphatic assertion that he had looked
everywhere. For the first few moments I had
no success ; then I bethought myself of the
extra pocket I had sewn in a thick waistcoat,
the very one he had worn the day we came
aboard. Sure enough there was the wallet,

together with two letters I had entrusted him to post for me a few days ago. I sat down to consider the situation, and was mean enough to seize my advantage. When I handed him the wallet, I made light of my finding that, but reproached him bitterly for his neglect in posting my two letters. One of these I declared to be most important. As I expected, he forgot the fact of my triumph ; scarcely asking me where I had discovered the wallet, he was all contrition regarding the letters. He would wire to my mother directly he got ashore—would that do ? I pretended to be greatly worried and concerned for some moments, then I assured him that a wire would be quite all right. His next move was even to me totally unexpected. He came into my cabin the next night and announced the fact that after all we should have to " hang out somewhere " till he could get some money telegraphed from England. Out of gratitude for the recovery of the wallet, he had used most of its contents in tipping the crew. " Did I not approve ? "

I X

" CHANCE," " VICTORY," AND SUCCESS

I THINK we were glad to be home once more, and we settled down to work in earnest for the next few months. My walking powers got less and less, and we were full of apprehension. We had by this time left our old house, Pent Farm, Kent. I used to tease Conrad often about his one and only adventure—alone—in taking a house. Having a small child of thirteen months old, I had impressed upon my husband the necessity of a provision of milk being easily available. His report on his return, after he had viewed the house three times, was that there was everything I could wish for—a whole drove of cows on the farm (we were only renting the farmhouse). In due course I arrived, very hot and tired, and some lucky instinct led me to call at the grocer's on my way from the station and make some few small purchases, among them a half-bottle of champagne, and, in case

the milking hour was late, a tin of milk.   When
we drove into the yard—a very unprepossessing
yard—terribly dusty on this hot afternoon, and
holding a sure promise of abundant mud a little
later in the year, my heart sank.   The well
was dry, as it was being cleaned out, and some
fifteen ugly big pigs had invaded my kitchen.
Ugh !   I cast my eyes across the meadows at
the side in search of the cows.   Truly a fine
drove, twenty or more—and every one a bullock !
There was, literally, not one cow on the place;
we had to send two miles and a half to get any
milk at all.   If we needed a messenger to take
a wire we had to hire a farm-cart at half a
crown to go to the nearest town, Luton.   This
really tried my fortitude, but at the same time
I excused my husband ;   I did not expect him
to know a cow from a bullock.   Joseph Conrad
was Joseph Conrad, and although he frequently
declared, in a somewhat aggrieved manner,
that he had managed to conduct his life by
himself till he reached the age of thirty-eight,
I maintained that he was not a practical
person—certainly not in domestic matters.

He discussed " Under Western Eyes " with
me more than any of the other novels.   He
even insisted that I should rehearse the scene
of the woman with the cat.   All the characters
in this novel were intimate acquaintances of

my imagination.   Just as this book was finished,
my husband had a very serious illness. We
lived then in one of two tiny cottages—the one
on the other side of the road was full of furniture
—in the pretty little village of Aldington. Mr.
Arthur Marwood lived two and a half miles
away. His friendship meant a great deal to
my husband. His sane judgment and shrewd
foresight made him a stimulating companion.
His death came as a great shock, and I recall
Conrad's sensitive reluctance to answer his
last summons when he lay dying. That reluctance was so characteristic; it always cost him
an awful effort to bring himself face to face
with suffering in any form. I had not left my
room for more than a month, and we had no
car of our own, but I accompanied him, and we
made the journey in a hired car. It was at
such times of stress that I found how much my
husband depended on me.

"Under Western Eyes" was, as it were, the
kernel of many happenings. The day Conrad
took the pile of manuscript to London marked
the beginning of much misfortune, and was
attended by three worrying little episodes.
He started to drive the two miles to the station
with our old gardener in a tiny governess-car.
Exasperated and terribly irritable, he drove
carelessly over a bump in the road and broke

a spring in the cart ; not realising his nervous
strength, he sat in a big arm-chair at his pub-
lishers and forced the back out of it ; and he
ended the day by pushing the foot out of the
bed in which he slept that night. This excess
of nervous strength brought its usual consequences, added to the fact that in his exasperation he had managed to quarrel violently, and
seriously, with a very old and tried friend.
That night was a very disturbed one, and the
next morning it was very plain that something
much more serious was wrong than a passing
attack of gout. My husband's voice, as he gave
directions for a doctor to be called at once,
alarmed me by its strangeness, particularly as
only a moment before he had forbidden me to
send for our medical man. I followed him into
a tiny room on the top of the stairs, where he
had thrown himself on a narrow bed, with not
a little apprehension. Clearly he was very ill,
and it behoved me not to allow my alarm to
appear in my face. This was the time for
rapid action. The doctor—he happened not
to be the man we usually had, but his partner
—refused to take the responsibility of removing
the invalid to another room. His temperature
was very high, but instinct told me I must act
at once. Accordingly I had a bed put in the
largest room, where so much of the book had

been written, protected the narrow wooden sides of the fireplace with some slabs of slate, and with the aid of two farm-labourers carried him into it. Then began weeks of nursing and anxiety. As usual he rambled all the time in his native tongue, except when he repeated over and over the Burial Service, while the bell in the church a few yards away tolled for the passing of some other troubled soul. Many times I stood at that window watching the dawn break and listening to his quiet voice repeating those solemn words over and over again. I vowed I would never again live so close to a church. (And yet our next home shared the churchyard wall as a boundary line with our garden !) Then came a night which will live in my mind for ever—a night whose slowly passing hours were fraught with an agony of apprehension. Once again I found myself face to face with a situation in which I must act with speed and instant decision. The local doctor, to whom I sent an urgent message at two o'clock in the morning, never appeared till long after eight—owing to some silly professional jealousy, I discovered later. I waited, watching my husband, and feeling more and more my helplessness. I knew from my messenger that he had been at home when my summons reached him, and at last I could bear it no longer. I mixed some whisky and hot water, and, passing my arm under his head, I coaxed him to swallow it, sip by sip; then I helped him to turn a little on his side, and stood by, holding my breath. Presently he fell into a fitful sleep, which became more and more sound; and finally, as the clock struck eight, the doctor rang the bell. I met the man at the door but refused to allow him to see my patient. His angry assertion that the responsibility was entirely mine I could afford to pass over; Conrad was sleeping peacefully, and my own doctor was already on the way. His approbation was very soothing, but my nerves were getting shaky after my long vigils night after night. Then followed weeks and weeks of convalescence. Nursing a child, you can do mostly what you will with it; nursing a woman is often difficult; but to nurse an artist, whose imagination is at the best of times over excitable, is very hard. Often have I laboriously dragged him in his chair across the room, only to see him run back to bed when he heard the doctor's car coming down the hill.

" A Personal Record " would have had a successor if Conrad had lived only a few more years. Much of the material for it we had discussed only a few days before his death. " Prince Roman " was to be included, as being in every way personal. He had the intention of including some of his very early experiences before he left Poland. Our recent visit to his native country had refreshed his memories.

The title of " 'Twixt Land and Sea" was the subject of some argument, as another book had just appeared, "'Twixt Sand and Sea." The first story, "A Smile of Fortune," was largely founded on fact—Joseph Conrad's one and only bargain. He used to accuse me of being jealous of Alice. That deal in potatoes must have been as great a surprise to him, in spite of anything he might say about his business capacity. In the early days of our married life he would often declare himself sagacious. The queer little trick he had of laying his forefinger along his nose as he made the assertion always amused me. My morning greeting was usually (if he happened to be in a good mood) a quotation from one of his books, " How goes it, you old image?"

Two amusing little incidents will show that both boys began to understand their father's ways when they were very young. Once, when Borys was three, he had been forbidden by Conrad to come upstairs to me while I was dressing. Apparently his need of me was too great, for he appeared at the bedroom door. Conrad chased him down into the dining-room, looking like business, to say the least of it. The boy darted behind a big chair and said, " Wait just a minute, Dada." It was impossible not to laugh at the child's precaution while he explained why he had disobeyed. John, when about the same age, had been observing his father dressing; he rushed down to me with this remark, " Good morning, Mum! I can't stop a minute. Dada's brushed his hair three times already." He had observed that brushing his hair many times was a sure sign of irritation on his father's part.

I once reproached my husband for never having told me the story of " The Secret Sharer." He laughingly assured me that so much of the actual story was pure fiction, invented on the spur of the moment, that there was very little real incident to tell.

" Freya of the Seven Isles " was a great favourite with us both, and I remember his coming to me and asking me if a girl would be likely to smack a man's face as Freya did Heemskirk's. There is something so pathetic in the whole story—pathetic and yet so faithful to real life—that it even now makes the tears come into my eyes. As the author says in his " Notes on My Books," this book of short stories ushered in a better period in the history of his writings. As short stories I think they

are perfect as to length and treatment, of just
the length to stimulate interest without dis-
appointing it.   Neither do either of them give
the impression of being cut to measure.   I don't
think Conrad ever conceived his books as
wholes before he began to write.   I remember
we had many long talks about the title of
" Chance," and for some time it " hung in the
wind," to use an expression he was fond of.
In his note to this book he shows, I think, a
certain dissatisfaction with the completed work
—a mood that I knew so well (his second reading
mood, as I used to call it).   Always at the second
reading of anything he had written he would
show much irritation and discontent with it.
It did not comfort him to argue against this
impression of the moment.   I would listen
sympathetically, point out what passage had
especially pleased me, quote a sentence here
and there—and wait.   After all, " Chance "
was the first book that really made a popular
stir, and a great part of this wide success was
due to Sir Hugh Clifford's friendly interest.

The four stories of " Within the Tides " are
all so different in character and treatment that I
protested at the time against their appearing
in the same volume.   As Joseph Conrad says
himself in his note to these stories: " A reviewer observed that I liked to write of men

who go to sea or live on lonely islands, un-
trammelled by the pressure of worldly circumstances, because such characters allowed freer
play to my imagination, which in their case
was only bounded by natural laws and the
universal human conventions." Such a criticism seems rather beside the mark in view of
the success of " Chance " and other stories
placed in less remote surroundings. Perhaps
the " Planter of Malata " is the most remote,
but the Moorsom family is surely sufficiently
conventional. " The Partner " is told in rather
a rollicking style—rare indeed with Conrad—
in the mood that is connected in my mind with
his funny little habit of laying his finger against
his nose ; he called it being sagacious. I first
heard the story as it was told by my husband
to a very old friend. Cloete was known to both
of them intimately. I used to enjoy sitting
sewing in a corner of the room, while Mr. Hope
and Joseph Conrad had what they called a good
yarn. I knew enough sailor terms to understand their language, and now and then I
would throw in a remark or ask some question.
All the seamen who occurred in those yarns
were known to me by name, and most of their
histories were perfectly familiar. " The Inn
of the Two Witches " : for sheer horror the
last two tales in this volume remind me of

some of those of Edgar Allan Poe. I could not sleep for nights after I had copied this story; it fascinated me beyond anything. I could not put it down. " Because of the Dollars " is also gruesome, but shows Captain Davidson as a true humanitarian. It ought to make a wonderful film, or, I should say, will make one, for I believe they will all one day be shown on the screen.

" Victory " was the last novel he wrote before the war ; the last word was written on the 29th of May 1914. And that last word was the title, " Victory." As Conrad says in his note on this book, he had an idea of changing the title ; he feared that it might be misleading ; people might think the novel had some bearing on the war. I remember the day so well that this novel was finished. He had been having many troubled days fighting his way to the end of it. He had been very erratic, and had taken his meals mostly alone for two or three weeks. I had been forced to warn callers off, for although he would hardly have been aware of them, there was the possibility that he would need my presence or would wander in search of me, insufficiently clad—at least for visitors. I was feeling the strain little less than he, and the day on which the last words were added, I had gone into the garden, finding it impossible to rest in the house. I stood talking to the old gardener in low tones, when the window above me was thrown violently open and Conrad thrust his head out. His voice was hoarse, and his appearance dishevelled ; the gardener lifted a scared face. " She's dead, Jess ! " " Who ? " I asked, suddenly feeling sick. " Why, Lena, of course, and I have got the title : it is ' Victory.' " He flung his cigarette out of the window and muttered the injunction, " Don't come near me. I am going to lie down."

It was more than two hours before I ventured to disturb him with the post and a dainty tea-tray. The room—it was our only spare one— was littered with papers that stirred uneasily as I opened the door. More than one cigarette had burnt itself out on the table at the head of the bed, and one still smouldered in a deep ash-tray by his side, full of stumps. I was thankful that he had for once used this receptacle. Later, in deference to my repeated entreaties, he consented to have water in a deep jar beside him. It was often my experience to be wakened suddenly by the flare of the book he had been reading, the pages of which had caught the flame of the candle beside him. I don't think I ever slept so soundly as to be unaware in an instant of anything unusual, or of the faintest smell of burning. Once, when he

was using a room alone, we, the maid and I,
made a strange discovery when we went to make
the bed. Somehow, during the night, he must
have knocked the candle out of the stick into his
bed, alight. A thick cake of candle-grease held
the bedclothes closely together. He became
very irate when I pointed this out to him when
he returned from the bathroom, and he insisted
that we must have knocked the candle into the
bed when he was not there. It was not until
I produced his discarded vests, also firmly
stuck together with grease, that he would admit
the possibility that it had happened in his
sleep. It was a great comfort when he had a
house with electric light. Three times I have
known him stand with his back to a gas-stove
and only move away when the back was burnt
out of his dressing-gown.

When " Victory " was dramatised by Mr.
Macdonald Hastings, I had to submit to being
dressed up as Lena, and once again I read aloud
to him each part.

Conrad's dread of being accused of becoming
in the least commonplace led him to feel not
a little anxious about what might be said of
this book. I believe he would have been
happier if he could have kept much of what he
wrote from being published. Often he would
declare that he would never write another line,

10

but I knew the worth of that statement. He could not have kept from writing even had he been blessed with enough of this world's goods as to have made writing unnecessary. Some of the early fragments of his manuscripts would be valuable to-day. I do not refer to the complete ones, bought by Mr. John Quinn, but to greatly treasured fragments bearing on their wide margins some queer little sketches of human faces, allegorical designs, coiled ropes, anchors,. and capstans. I had quite a pile of loose pages with designs, and I left a tearful request that my box containing them should remain unopened during my enforced stay in the nursing - home. As I spent the first six months after my return home upstairs in my room, I did not miss my treasures for a long time. My inquiries met with a somewhat curt reply that " all that was of any value amongst that rubbish was locked in the study drawers." As far as I have been able to ascertain since, the only thing he thought worth preserving was the manuscript of the " Black Mate," now in the possession of Mr. T. J. Wise. But I still have some twelve or thirteen sketches in red and black ink. These little pictures, drawn on single sheets of soiled note-paper, I boldly rescued from a cupboard in his study when Conrad was absent in America.

" An Arrow of Gold " seems to belong more to me than any of the others, inasmuch that had it not been for me, it would certainly never have been written. One morning Conrad was thrashing himself to pieces because his mind was, as he said, a blank. The story I had heard many times before, even during our honeymoon. Fearful of saying one word too much, I ventured to recall just one episode to his mind. Many times I have written down some few facts, an incident or two, which I had thought might bring his thoughts into train. These efforts on my part were never successful. He would glance at them, sometimes write a few lines on the paper, while I would stand hopefully by ; then, with a gesture of exasperation, he would thrust the paper into my hand and say impatiently, " Why don't you write the thing yourself ? You could do it quite well ; everything essential is there." Write it myself ! Yes, I often felt like trying. But the certainty that he would only place the result in a drawer and turn the key on it when I had finished, restrained me. Those few little articles I wrote, which appeared in the *Daily Mail*, were written and sent off without his knowledge. I shall not forget the first time he read one of them printed in his morning paper. I think the days when I had been guilty of writing were the only ones when we were both acutely conscious that there was something hidden between us. I must have betrayed myself by a feeling of exultation I always found it so difficult to hide. My recollections of " The Rescue " were printed in a number of the *Bookman's Journal*, as also the truth about " The Nature of a Crime," and the history of the two little notebooks containing the " Congo Diary."

Turning over a box of papers a few days ago, I came upon the first draft of " The Rescue " —a pile of close-typed sheets corrected in the hand of the author more than twenty-eight years ago. Very different is the finished book to those early pages—pages I loved to type. The poetic quality of these pages reveals Conrad in quite a different mood to that in which he wrote the version which now stands as the book. There is only one other piece of writing of Joseph Conrad that holds that particular quality : an unfinished manuscript called " The Sisters." The haunting cadence of both these MSS. had a charm for me none of the later work had, notwithstanding the fact that all critics would say they were immature. Joseph Conrad was not fond of verse. I can only remember two books of verse that earned his approval. One written by a young Frenchman, and the

other by a friend, Mr. Arthur Symons. My
husband often lamented his inability to appreciate verse and his indifferent sense of smell.
These pages of " The Rescue," discoloured and
crumpled though they may be, are still perfectly
legible. I remember the great day when the
book was begun ; my preparations for this
great undertaking ; Joseph Conrad's frequent
visits to the little room where I sat at work.
He was quite as excited as I was, and, looking
back, I rather think he retarded my progress in
typing them, in spite of his repeated words of
encouragement. He wrote quite a considerable amount before he laid the book aside. I
used at last to have an uncomfortable feeling
that a run of ill-luck would only change when
that manuscript should be finished. Finally, in
1919, the first instalment appeared in *Land and
Water*. I remember his reluctance to take up
the story again ; he seemed to think he would
never be able to hide the join. To me it is
remarkable that he could ever again capture
the mood. I am thankful I persuaded Conrad
not to allow Ford Madox Hueffer to assist in
the finishing. It appeared a sacrilege to me.
I don't doubt that the offer was made in all
good faith and friendliness—for those were the
days when the two were friends—but the fact
remains that I could not endure the idea.

Some months before the book was finished, Conrad brought me a sealed envelope in which was a slip of paper with the actual last two words written on it—" Steer north." I had to make him a solemn promise not to open the envelope till after the book was finished. I still treasure that envelope.

X

LAST STORIES

THE appearance of the little book, " The Nature of a Crime," has caused so much comment, so much speculation, that perhaps these few words of explanation will not come amiss. Assertions have been made that the book was a recent collaboration between Ford Madox Hueffer and my husband. Very little of this " fragment " belongs to Conrad. Even that little had passed so completely out of his mind that when once I showed him the typed pages, which I had for many years in my possession, he disclaimed all knowledge of it. He said, in fact, that the thing had been sent him by some complete stranger and directed me to destroy it.

The statement made in a recent copy of the *Literary Digest*, New York, that " several decades ago it was published in an obscure little journal " is hardly correct. It appeared in two of the early numbers of *The English Review*.

In 1924, when Mr. Hueffer unearthed the " Nature of a Crime," Conrad refused to admit that he had ever heard of it. It was not until I discovered the two numbers of the *Review* that he could be made to believe in the existence of the printed pages. He then declared it to be too trivial to be reprinted, and he only yielded to Mr. Hueffer's request to be allowed to publish in the *Transatlantic*, "because," as he said, " he was tired of argument."

I suggested that he should permit Mr. Hueffer to reprint it under his own name alone. Recalling Mr. Hueffer's recent statements as to his being always the lion's share in collaboration, one would have expected him to have jumped at the idea ; but of course there was magic in the name of Joseph Conrad. Turning out some papers of manuscript in my husband's desk a few months ago, I came upon some few pages of this very " fragment," written in my husband's hand.

" Autocracy and War," written in 1905 and printed in the *Fortnightly Review*, was another thing that my husband refused to admit as written by him. My efforts to convince him ended in what he considered a victory, a walk-over for him. I was silenced, but only for a while. The late Mr. J. B. Pinker had in his office unquestionable proofs, sufficiently convincing even for Conrad.

The friendship between Mr. J. B. Pinker and my husband was an old and tried one. We had seen a lot of Mr. Pinker of recent years. His unexpected death was a great blow to us both, and we appreciated very much the thoughtful kindness on the part of his sons, who motored so many miles to break the sad news in person. Conrad remarked, and I fancy I hear his voice now, " And J. B. promised always to see me off, and be a friend to you."

" The Short Diary," which has appeared in " Last Essays," was written in pencil in two little sixpenny notebooks with shiny black covers. They must have been in some queer places. My husband has told me he often thought he had lost them, as he took no particular care of them. He regarded his diary in the light of a friendly listener, and it comforted him often in his loneliness, on the march or in camp. Tossed carelessly into an old metal explorer's trunk, that trunk eventually turned up in France on our honeymoon. It also contained, beside one or two seafaring papers, two greatly discoloured cotton pillow-cases. I was inclined to relegate these latter to the rag-bag, but something restrained me, and they afterwards formed a sling for the poor gout-tortured hand, at a time when nothing else was available. Conrad wanted to burn the papers forthwith.

I was too timid in those days to protest, and they owed their preservation to the appearance of a chance visitor, who distracted him.

The pains taken by Mr. Richard Curle, who patiently copied them, and his sympathetic introduction, makes the little diary a delightful whole. None can fail to recognise in those short, terse sentences the familiar spirit of the author, more perhaps his spoken than his written style.

Often in later years would Conrad attempt to write on odd pieces of paper in remote corners of the garden. Once he even annexed the only bathroom we had. He would give no reason for his strange choice, but for over a week our bathing hours were greatly restricted. In another phase he would wear only a greatly faded bath-robe, and insisted on working in the conservatory which adjoined the drawing-room. This necessitated posting a maid as scout near the front door to warn me of intending callers. I fancy the old gardener was the principle sufferer at this time. The expression of his gloomy face when he caught sight of the yellow-striped bath-robe tempted me always to laugh outright. Conrad often declared that he detested his study, but I noticed he was never at ease unless his familiar books were at hand. A cigarette burn usually adorned their covers, and I have suffered if the books happened to belong to some one else. Sheets and table-linen were hall-marked in the same manner. A word from me calling attention to the fact never failed to produce the same answer: " Well, my dear, it's done. No use crying over spilt milk. I will buy you another ! "

He had often the most fantastic notions about one's motives, and he would attribute the most far-fetched reasons for anything unexpected. At first I was not a little disconcerted, and more than once I have been greatly troubled at having to explain some trivial occurrence. It generally ended up by his exclaiming with a shrug of his shoulders, " That's so like you English ! " My usual retort was " Stupid British subject ! "

Now, as I sit here alone, these little remembrances flash through my mind, and perhaps one feels for a moment that in some cases one may have been a little impatient or at some time invested trifles with undue importance.

" The Rover " has been called, perhaps with justice, the most finished of all Conrad's works. Its reception, even while it pleased him, also vexed him, because it had been better received than " The Rescue." I used to laugh and tell him that he was like a jealous parent, watchful for some slight on a favourite child. I have in my possession a wonderful little sketch he made on an old envelope unearthed from his writing-table. It is only a face—the face of an old French shell-back, as he would affectionately have called him—his own conception of " Old Peyrol." So many of his friends tried to appease him, and pointed out the many merits of the book. The fact that both books were his own creation failed to console him. His dissatisfaction with that book seems strangely pathetic in view of its containing those wonderful lines of Spenser's that are now engraven on the stone which marks his resting-place. No other lines could have been more appropriate, or have conveyed so clearly the feeling of us all. I feel that he might even have chosen them himself.

I have a deep feeling of gratitude to all of those friends who have written so tenderly and sympathetically about him, who have shown in their delicate references their true regard for the man who has lived in their midst. Among these there are a few who have expressed the sentiments I and the boys have been unable to find fitting words to express.

For all that has been written I have felt the greatest gratitude, though gratitude is perhaps not quite the word to use. I might say I have felt the greatest pride in these written words of

appreciation of Conrad as an author and of
tender regret for him as a man. The essay
written by his old and valued friend, Mr.
Cunninghame Graham, which was printed in
the *Saturday Review* (16th August 1924), is
the most beautiful of all. With his wonderful
clearness of vision he has made it possible for
others to follow the sorrowful procession through
the old town, almost step by step. One feels
that in spite of the fact that the modern motor
replaced the dignity of a horse-drawn hearse,
the cortège passed unhurried. I cannot forbear
quoting the following passage :

" . . . The rain had cleared and the sun
poured down upon us, as in procession, headed
by the acolytes and priests, we bore the coffin
to the grave. The semi-circle of Scotch firs
formed, as it were, a little harbour for him.
The breeze blew freshly south-west by south a
little westerly—a good wind, as I thought, to
steer up Channel by, and one that he who would
no longer feel it on his cheek, looking aloft to
see that the sails were drawing properly, must
have been glad to carry when he struck sound-
ings, passing the Wolf Rock or the Smalls after
foul weather in the Bay.

" Handsomely, as he who lay in it might
well have said, they lowered the coffin down.
The priest had left his Latin and said a prayer

or two in English, and I was glad of it, for English surely was the speech the Master Mariner most loved, and honoured in the loving with new graces of his own.

" The voyage was over and the great spirit rested from its toil, safe in the English earth that he had dreamed of as a child in far Ukrainia. A gleam of sun lit up the red brick houses of the town. It fell upon the tower of the cathedral, turning it into a glowing beacon pointing to the sky. The trees moved gently in the breeze, and in the fields the ripening corn was undulating softly, just as the waves waft in on an atoll in the Pacific, with a slight swishing sound. All was well chosen for his resting-place, and so we left him with his sails all duly furled, ropes flemished down, and with the anchor holding truly in the kind Kentish earth, until the Judgment Day. The gulls will bring him tidings as they fly past above his grave, with their wild voices, if he should weary for the sea and the salt smell of it."

It hardly seems possible that it is only a year and a half ago since I watched that procession, winding its way through the park, from his study windows, preceded by a police cyclist to clear the way, and with the sun peeping fitfully through the clouds scudding across the sky. My sorrowing fancy kept pace with it long,

long after a turn in the road had hidden it from my sight. Mr. Cunninghame Graham's words fitted exactly with my mental picture. Canterbury cricket week, Canterbury's gayest moment, and that one loved human being passing through on his last journey in solemn contrast !

The " Tales of Hearsay " are four stories that belong to long ago, to the days when I used to copy his manuscript. I am certain that he would not have included in this volume the story, " Prince Roman," had he lived. It was of this very story we had been speaking only the day before the day he was taken ill. He said then that he would write another book of Reminiscences. " ' Prince Roman ' will go quite well into that book, Jess, and I have quite enough material to make a second. Fortunately the form will not prevent me from publishing another volume, and call it ' Further Reminiscences.' "

Then comes " Suspense "—which because of its unfinished state leaves us in " suspense." Three names were mentioned as men who might have been induced to finish it. Without any personal prejudice on my part, I maintain that it would have been *impossible for any living man* to have finished this book. Even his most intimate friends had no notion of the end. He told me once that he had quite half a dozen different ways to bring it to an end. I know that he intended cutting it down—the part that now stands as the book—in a most ruthless manner. He had, in fact, already weeded out whole slabs that would have been used, no doubt in the main, though not perhaps quite in the form it was previously written.

There has been much comment on Conrad's interest in Napoleon. Considering that several of his maternal relations were officers in Napoleon's army, and that his paternal grandfather was also a General at the time of his death, one might almost say that it was inherited. General Korzeniowski, his grandfather, dismounted from his horse, feeling unwell, and died quietly leaning by its side. His medals, together with one or two other precious relics, came to us in a little sealed packet in 1919 or 1920. Among these were a bundle of old letters, Conrad's own mother's wedding-ring, bearing the date 1856 and the name Evelina, and two scarf-pins. A melancholy little packet, preserved by some strange fate, retrieved by the same mysterious fate, to find a home at last in a little old Florentine box in an English drawing-room.

I will quote a passage from the " Reminiscences " to show that Conrad's interest in

Napoleon was not equivalent to a liking for the man or admiration for his character. I remember hearing the story to which it refers, before we were married : of his great loathing and disgust when he first heard that a grand-uncle, during the retreat from Moscow, had been so hard pressed by hunger that he, with one or two other officers, had made a meal of " a luckless Lithuanian dog." " An extreme distaste for that objectionable episode has tinged the views I hold as to the character and achievements of Napoleon the Great. I need not say that these are unfavourable. It was morally reprehensible for that great captain to induce a simple-minded Polish gentleman to eat dog, by raising in his breast a false hope of national inde-pendence. It has been the fate of that credulous nation to starve for upwards of a hundred years on a diet of false hopes and—well, dog ! "

Soon will follow that big book, " Life and Letters of Conrad " ; a book that must be a monument of fact—facts that another friend, M. Jean Aubry, has collected and verified with the most patient care, visiting every place for authentic information. Much of this book will be new even to me, in spite of the fact that I have retained a vivid recollection of all Conrad has ever told me of his childhood, and in spite of the many things that his nearest relatives have told me at different times. When all these facts are printed, and all is known of this great man of letters, to most he will appear more strange, more complex, than ever. The choice of the sea as a profession will be difficult to understand, his love for his adopted country, and his understanding of her people.

Now that this little book is finished—finished but leaving so much unsaid—I feel that, although much will be written about him, in admiration of his work, in criticism of its style, favourable and unfavourable, yet this is the only book that can be written about his private life ; the most human, because the most intimate, account of him.